The Angel and the Perverts

The Cutting Edge
Lesbian Life and Literature
Series Editor: *Karla Jay*
PROFESSOR OF ENGLISH AND WOMEN'S STUDIES
PACE UNIVERSITY

Elizabeth Wood
Musicologist and Writer
Committee on Theory and Culture
New York University

Bonnie Zimmerman
Women's Studies
San Diego State University

The Cutting Edge:
Lesbian Life and Literature
Series Editor: Karla Jay

The Angel
and the Perverts

Lucie Delarue-Mardrus

translated by Anna Livia

New York University Press
NEW YORK
AND LONDON

NEW YORK UNIVERSITY PRESS
New York and London

Library of Congress Cataloging-in-Publication Data
Delarue-Mardrus, Lucie, 1875-1945.
[Ange et les pervers. English]
The angel and the perverts / Lucie Delarue-Mardrus ; translated by
Anna Livia.
p.   cm.—(The cutting edge—lesbian life and literature)
Includes bibliographical references.
ISBN 0-8147-5080-X (cloth : alk. paper).—ISBN 0-8147-5098-2
(paper : alk. paper)
I. Livia, Anna.   II. Title.   III. Series: Cutting edge (New York,
N.Y.)
PQ2607.E24A713   1995
843'.912—dc20   95-15342
CIP

New York University Press books are printed on acid-free paper,
and their binding materials are chosen for strength and durability.

Manufactured in the United States of America

10   9   8   7   6   5   4   3   2   1

Contents

Foreword

Despite the efforts of lesbian and feminist publishing houses and a few university presses, the bulk of the most important lesbian works has traditionally been available only from rare-book dealers, in a few university libraries, or in gay and lesbian archives. This series intends, in the first place, to make representative examples of this neglected and insufficiently known literature available to a broader audience by reissuing selected classics and by putting into print for the first time lesbian novels, diaries, letters, and memoirs that are of special interest and significance, but which have moldered in libraries and private collections for decades or even for centuries, known only to the few scholars who had the courage and financial wherewithal to track them down.

Their names have been known for a long time—Sappho, the Amazons of North Africa, the Beguines, Aphra Behn, Queen Christina, Emily Dickinson, the Ladies of Llangollen, Radclyffe Hall, Natalie Clifford Barney, H.D., and so many others from every nation, race, and era. But government

and religious officials burned their writings, historians and
literary scholars denied they were lesbians, powerful men
kept their books out of print, and influential archivists
locked up their ideas far from sympathetic eyes. Yet some
dedicated scholars and readers still knew who they were,
made pilgrimages to the cities and villages where they had
lived and to the graveyards where they rested. They passed
around tattered volumes of letters, diaries, and biographies,
in which they had underlined what seemed to be telltale hints
of a secret or different kind of life. Where no hard facts
existed, legends were invented. The few precious and often
available pre-Stonewall lesbian classics, such as *The Well of
Loneliness* by Radclyffe Hall, *The Price of Salt* by Claire
Morgan (Patricia Highsmith), and *Desert of the Heart* by
Jane Rule, were cherished. Lesbian pulp was devoured. One
of the primary goals of this series is to give the more neglected works, which constitute the vast majority of lesbian
writing, the attention they deserve.

A second but no less important aim of this series is to
present the "cutting edge" of contemporary lesbian scholar-
ship and theory across a wide range of disciplines. Prac-
titioners of lesbian studies have not adopted a uniform approach to literary theory, history, sociology, or any other
discipline, nor should they. This series intends to present an
array of voices that truly reflects the diversity of the lesbian
community. To help me in this task, I am lucky enough to be
assisted by a distinguished editorial board that reflects various professional, class, racial, ethnic, and religious back-
grounds as well as a spectrum of interests and sexual preferences.

At present the field of lesbian studies occupies a small,

precarious, and somewhat contested pied-à-terre between gay studies and women's studies. The former is still in its infancy, especially if one compares it to other disciplines that have been part of the core curriculum of every child and adolescent for several decades or even centuries. However, although it is one of the newest disciplines, gay studies may also be the fastest-growing one—at least in North America. Lesbian, gay, and bisexual studies conferences are doubling and tripling their attendance. Although only a handful of degree-granting programs currently exists, the number is also apt to multiply quickly during the next decade.

In comparison, women's studies is a well-established and burgeoning discipline with hundreds of minors, majors, and graduate programs throughout the United States. Lesbian Studies occupies a peripheral place in the discourse in such programs, characteristically restricted to one lesbian-centered course, usually literary or historical in nature. In the many women's studies series that are now offered by university presses, generally only one or two books on a lesbian subject or issue are included, and lesbian voices are restricted to writing on those topics considered of special interest to gay people. We are not called upon to offer opinions on motherhood, war, education, or on the lives of women not publicly identified as lesbians. As a result, lesbian experience is too often marginalized and restricted.

In contrast, this series will prioritize, centralize, and celebrate lesbian visions of literature, art, philosophy, love, religion, ethics, history, and myriad other topics. In "The Cutting Edge," readers can find authoritative versions of important lesbian texts that have been carefully prepared and introduced by scholars. Readers can also find the work of academics and independent scholars who write about other aspects of life from a distinctly lesbian viewpoint. These visions are not only various but intentionally contradictory, for lesbians speak from differing class, racial, ethnic, and religious perspectives. Each author also speaks from and about a certain moment of time, and few would argue that being a lesbian today is the same as it was for Sappho or Anne Lister. Thus no attempt has been made to homogenize that diversity, and no agenda exists to attempt to carve out a "politically correct" lesbian studies perspective at this juncture in history or to pinpoint the "real" lesbians in history. It seems more important for all the voices to be heard before those with the blessings of aftersight lay the mantle of authenticity on any one vision of the world, or on any particular set of women.

What each work in this series does share, however, is a common realization that gay women are the "Other" and that one's perception of culture and literature is filtered by sexual behaviors and preferences. Those perceptions are not the same as those of gay men or of nongay women, whether the writers speak of gay or feminist issues or whether the writers choose to look at nongay figures from a lesbian perspective. The role of this series is to create space and give a voice to those interested in lesbian studies. This series speaks to any person who is interested in gender studies, literary criticism, biography, or important literary works, whether she or he is a student, professor, or serious reader, for the series is neither for lesbians only nor even by lesbians only. Instead, "The Cutting Edge" attempts to share some of the best of lesbian literature and lesbian studies with anyone willing to look at the world through lesbians' eyes. The series is proactive in that it will help to formulate and foreground the very discipline on which it focuses. Finally, this series has answered the call to make lesbian theory, lesbian experience, lesbian lives, lesbian literature, and lesbian visions the heart and nucleus, the weighty planet around which for once other viewpoints will swirl as moons to our earth. We invite readers of all persuasions to join us by venturing into this and other books in this series.

The first translation into English of Lucie Delarue-Mardrus's *The Angel and the Perverts* is a charming addition to this series. Delarue-Mardrus's novel about the hermaphrodite Mario/Marion belongs to an entire category of French Literature from the turn of the century to approximately 1930 which depicted lesbians as members of a "third sex." The hermaphrodite became the visual representation of the ways in which lesbians were "different" from their heterosexual sisters, and Renée Vivien, Natalie Clifford Barney, Rachilde, and Colette, among others, shared Delarue-Mardrus's fascination with the topic. Delarue-Mardrus was an important author, whose work up until the publication of this volume has been relatively unknown and unavailable in English. In an important introduction, Anna Livia rereads Lucie Delarue-Mardrus as a prolific and significant writer, despite the fact that previous scholars viewed her primarily as the wife of the scholar and translator Joseph-Charles Mardrus. Livia also places Delarue-Mardrus's life in a lesbian context for the first time and decodes this delightful novel so that readers will feel quite at home in Mario/Marion's unusual world.

KARLA JAY
Professor of English and Women's Studies
Pau University

Acknowledgments

And this is where I thank the many people who helped with this project. First of all Deb Shoss, gifted with a ferociously keen eye for typos, who read and corrected each chapter and whose enthusiastic comments made rewriting easy; Karla Jay for insightful criticism, helpful suggestions, and amazingly prompt response time; Niko Pfund for his enthusiasm for the project; Kira Hall for acting as sounding board as I read her my day's work; Veronica O'Donovan for an informative discussion of the artistic sensibility of the period; Veronica O'Donovan and Kira Hall's kitchen table upon which the introduction was writ; Catherine Gonnard and Marie-Geneviève Havel for having me to stay in Paris while I did research for this book; Jean Chalon for graciously allowing us to reproduce the cover photograph of Lucie Delarue-Mardrus; and finally my mother, Dympna Monica Jones, for her wit, intelligence, and ironic turn of phrase, the three qualities which have made me what I am today.

Introduction:
Lucie Delarue-Mardrus and the
Phrenetic Harlequinade

Part One: Lucie Delarue-Mardrus[1]

Lucie Delarue-Mardrus was a phenomenally prolific writer, chalking up more than seventy books in her seventy-one years of life, including some forty-seven novels, twelve collections of poetry, and two film adaptations of her fiction. Yet nowadays her name is rarely mentioned unless in connection with that of her husband, Joseph-Charles Mardrus, translator of the Arabian Nights, and his distinguished circle of friends, which included most of literary Paris of the 1900s and the *années folles*. Indeed, it was her husband's frequent boast that he had made Lucie what she was, and in a joking divorce settlement, in which he lists all he had given her, he includes the name "Lucie Delarue-Mardrus," the development of her personality, the daily example of his own way of

life, her publishers, and the few decent friends who number
among the rest of her acquaintance (Plat 1994: 167–168).
These days Delarue-Mardrus's work itself is all but forgotten, save for the nostalgic wistfulness of the synesthetic first
line, "L'odeur de mon pays était dans une pomme" (In the
smell of an apple I held my native land), while few can
remember the rest of the poem.[2]

When Lucie Delarue-Mardrus was a young woman, the
Italian poet Gabriele D'Annunzio brought perfume he had
mixed specially for her. The sculptor Auguste Rodin was
extravagant in his praise of her physical beauty. Sarah Bernhardt kept a portrait Lucie had painted of her in her dressing
room. The symbolist Odilon Redon painted a picture inspired by her poetry. Belgian officials invited her to read a
poem she had composed for the King of Belgium's birthday.
In Beirut, the merchant Prince, Pharaon, threw roses, armfuls
of roses, the whole harvest of roses from his rose gardens in
Damascus, a year's worth of precious oil and rose essence,
into the wake of her departing ship. In 1919, she appeared
in *Le Tout Paris* as a famous personality (the equivalent of
being featured on the cover of *Time*); in 1922, she had a
total of eight requests for novels from such prominent French
journals as *Candide,* the *Revue de Paris, Intransigeant,* and
the *Journal.* She gave lecture tours in Belgium, Holland,
Denmark, England, Portugal, Brazil, and the United States.
Yet at her death at midnight, April 21, 1945, Lucie Delarue-
Mardrus was pretty much a pauper, dependent on the generosity of her friends and living on a small pension from the
Société des Gens de Lettres. In her last years her manuscripts
were sent back to her with depressing rapidity, her novel
Fleurette was banned by the Nazis, her *Poèmes mignons*

were removed from the school curriculum, and her work and opinions were attacked by the collaborationist paper *Je suis partout,* though she had never been prominent in any political context and her writing was considered more charming than radical.

Hers was not merely the ordinary decline of an elderly woman no longer in the public eye (and by "ordinary" I mean neither natural nor merited), nor the classic fall from favor of a child of the Victorian era in a nation which had seen two world wars, but the result of a quiet heroism, an unfailing loyalty to the woman she loved, despite family quarrels, the distaste of her publishers, the terrifying rise of anti-Semitism, and interrogation by the Gestapo during the Occupation. For, despite the fanfare of her marriage to Joseph-Charles (the initials "J.-C." were affectionately interpreted as an abbreviation for Jesus Christ by his friends and familiars), Lucie had always been primarily attracted to women. Other commentators have concentrated on discussing the Mardrus as a couple. Since the marriage was to last only fifteen years and, as I will argue, it was her women friends who had the greatest influence on Lucie, I prefer to trace her growing affection for women, rather than emphasize the importance of Joseph-Charles.

Born in 1874, the youngest of six sisters, daughters of a wealthy and successful shipping lawyer, Lucie Delarue-Mardrus spent an idyllic childhood in a mansion in Honfleur on the Normandy coast, surrounded by a green and expansive park of four hundred and forty acres, complete with dogs, goats, ducks, and a plentiful supply of English governesses. The six little girls (whose childhood is recaptured in Delarue-Mardrus's *Le Roman de six petites filles,* The novel of six little girls) were given the run of the estate, but forbidden to mix with other children even to the extent of sharing catechism lessons with the children of Honfleur. They grew up free-spirited but naive and almost completely ignorant of matters heterosexual.

The big events in Lucie's memoirs (which reads sometimes like a diary), the ones which she prefaces "In Provins an unexpected fairy tale awaited me" (Delarue-Mardrus 1938: 78) or "An important adventure awaited me when I returned from Vasouÿ" (ibid.), tell of her successes with men. She writes, for example, of her meeting with a young foreign composer who became her fiancé for a few weeks; the night she met the young Captain Pétain—he who was to become Maréchal Pétain, leader of collaborationist France—and went for a midnight walk with him while he called her his blue lotus; of her friendship with Gaston de B., who begged her to marry him.

Yet her descriptions of these men are cool, passionless compared with the feelings she expresses for the women she falls in love with. Gaston de B., for example, seemed more like a mentor than a sweetheart and often bored her. He was, in short, "a thrill-less companion" (92). Captain Pétain, despite his wide knowledge of art and music, apparently already had the cold look which was to characterize the Maréchal (110). Of her almost-fiancé she writes, "I was soon persuaded that I loved him" (85), this emotion being aroused by his virtuoso performance on the piano and his poetic poverty. One day, the two were alone together looking out at the waters of the estuary, when he took her gently by the shoulders and kissed her. Lucie, nineteen at the time, had been imagining this kiss since she was fifteen years old, sure that when it came it would make her faint with pleasure. Instead she felt nothing at all, but found the whole event uncomfortable, without pleasure or joy, and caught herself coldly looking on at the scene as though she were someone else. She remarks impersonally that the gesture was repeated several times during the season, and each time she felt less and less for the musician. She was relieved, therefore, when her father, discovering some mildly damning information about the young man's background, put an end to the relationship and sent the young man home. A very different impression this than her adoration, at the age of six, of a playmate's mother, who picked her up impetuously and set her on her lap. Writing her memoirs nearly sixty years later, although she cannot remember what the woman looked like, Lucie still feels the joy, complete, unique, and ecstatic of sitting on the woman's knee. She didn't ever want to get down. As her playmate called her away she felt an inconsolable sadness and reflects, "that was the first passion of my life" (Delarue-Mardrus 1938: 31).

When the fourteen-year-old daughter of some distant relatives came to stay at the family estate in Honfleur, Lucie listened with a mixture of horror and fascination to the details of what went on during the infamous wedding night. Though she learned all the words to the smutty songs her friend sang, put on make-up and tilted her beret at a rakish angle "so as to look like a tart," she seems to have avoided the heterosexual imperative inherent in these lessons. Instead she developed a crush on her friend's mother of the same intensity as the passion she had felt at six years old, and spent hours writing poems, which she never dared give her. When a quarrel blew up between the woman and Lucie's

mother, causing Lucie's love object to leave the estate, Lucie
was heartbroken. For a while. Until, at her sister's wedding
(a grand affair lasting three days), a strange woman guest
caught her attention, or rather, her imagination, and consoled her for the loss of her beloved.

Lucie describes these passions as strong but fleeting, one
passing fancy eclipsed by the next, and yet they caused her
considerable anguish and soul searching. At eighteen she
attended the Institut Normal Catholique in Paris with her
sister Georgina (who was later to become a nun) and hoped
that under the benign influence of the Catholic church she
would succeed in driving out her "bad thoughts" and em-
brace the faith. But, she notes, the despair remained. Instead,
she became infatuated with a friend of her sister Charlotte,
and turned her back on the morally improving literature she
should have been reading to write sonnets for her new idol
as she had before in Honfleur. This time she gathered up the
courage to give them to the woman for whom they were
written, but she, a cold Protestant, was markedly unenthusi-
astic.

This was not to be the end of the story, however, for the
cold Protestant came to visit Charlotte in Normandy and
Lucie discovered to her pleasure that the old infatuation was
still there. After dinner one night some of the girls took their
guest out into the fields so they could see the lights of Le
Havre twinkling in the distance. Waiting until she was as-
sured of secrecy in the sheltering dark of the trees, the cold
Protestant bent quickly over Lucie, who, thinking she wanted
to whisper something in her ear, leant toward her. Suddenly
she felt the other's lips on hers. This second kiss, so different
from the first offered by her designated suitor, which had left

her completely indifferent, moved her to the very core and nearly made her cry out. "Trembling, inflamed, this time it lived up to my dreams. I would have given my life itself for a second kiss like that" (Delarue-Mardrus 1938: 86). The Protestant, however, turned cold again and chatted animatedly with Lucie's sisters so that her young friend could not even take her arm.

These infatuations were, it seems, a training ground for Lucie's passion for Impéria de Heredia (wife of the poet José-Maria de Heredia), whose first words on seeing Lucie, then twenty-one years old, were the surprised exclamation, "Your daughter is simply ravishing!" (Delarue-Mardrus 1938: 99). Lucie was immediately smitten. Impéria, then in her forties, had grown up in diplomatic circles, spoke four or five languages, was cultured and artistic and of a long aristocratic lineage. For Lucie she represented poetry, mystery, beauty, nobility, pleasure, and romanticism: a powerful combination. Impéria and one of her daughters were invited to spend a fortnight at the Delarue estate and Lucie recounts how her father took a party of them out in the carriage to visit a *château* near one of his shoots. The day she spent in the company of this woman was to remain in Lucie's memory as one of the most emotional events of her life. The details still stand out in her mind forty years later, from the old *château* refurbished in a mock-medieval style, to the simple little church of Carbec, afternoon tea at a local farmer's, the washer-women beating their clothes down by the riverside, and Impéria's words in the carriage on the way home, "When evening falls, a kind of melancholy passes over. This little one is feeling that at this moment, I believe." Lucie even remembered the name of the farmer: "Dagoubert" she recalls proudly, and it is no surprise to learn that she rides down to Carbec every year to relive the memories of that day.

After many visits between the two families, there finally came a day when Lucie and Impéria found themselves alone together in the bedroom of the Parisian flat where Lucie slept with her mother and sister, Georgina. Impéria was sitting in a chair, Lucie was crouching in front of a chest of drawers, searching for something she wanted to show her. Suddenly Lucie turned aside and, finding herself kneeling before her, laid her arms in Impéria's lap and whispered, "I'm afraid of you!"

"Why?" asked Impéria, smiling.

In an even softer voice, Lucie murmured, "Because I'm afraid of loving you too much."

"You're afraid of loving me too much? One can never love too much. You . . ."

But she said no more because Lucie had thrown herself against her and Impéria kissed her passionately. A moment afterward, however, Impéria had withdrawn to a glacial distance, murmuring in horror, "What would your father say if he knew? He's just next door . . ." (Delarue-Mardrus 1938: 106). This muttered fear gave her away, however, for instead of the formal *vous* form she usually used when speaking to Lucie, in the heat of the moment she had said *tu*.

It was with a mixture of delight and terror in her heart that Lucie went out with her mother and sister Georgina that night, though she remembered nothing of the evening itself. She had heard the *tu* and it stirred her heart so much that she would close her eyes when she thought of it. Given the extreme formality of the upper class of the period, the little word *tu* acts as a declaration of love. Certainly Lucie experienced all the confused and conflicted emotions of first love, feeling like a marked woman, a lost soul damned by the Christian church, and yet at the same time as though she had just been born. She spent a sleepless night thinking of this passion for which she could dare anything: dishonor, prison, death, or murder. In the morning she wrote a poem for her beloved which she ran to the post office to mail. But, like the cold Protestant before her, Impéria made no comment, trying to pretend the incident had never taken place. Lucie was forced to keep her feelings to herself, though she later wrote of them in her novels *L'Acharnée* (The woman in hot pursuit) (1910) and *Le Beau Baiser* (The beautiful kiss) (1929). When the family returned to Normandy for the summer, Lucie took to wandering along the estuary for hours, barefoot, alone, and wearing only a navy blue smock and a necklace of rowan leaves. The images of the sea in *Occident,* her first collection of poetry, were composed during these days of gazing at the sand and the waves and thinking of Her.

On the fifth of June 1900, Lucie married Joseph-Charles Mardrus, translator of the Arabian Nights. Lucie had met Joseph-Charles at a dinner organized by her friend, Marie Bengesco, shortly after the family's return from their summer in Normandy, the summer Lucie had spent gloomily pacing the strand in her blue smock, thinking of Impéria. The day after this dinner, Joseph-Charles went to the Delarue house and asked her father for her hand in marriage, declaring Lucie to be, quite simply, "one of the best poets of the French language," though none of her poems had yet been published and he had heard them recited at dinner only. Where the Delarue family were staid and conventional, Lucie's husband-to-be was impulsive and eccentric. Unlike her sister, Charlotte, whose marriage took place with all due ceremony over three days on the family estate, Lucie was married, at her husband's orders, in the bicycling gear that was all the rage among the beautiful people of 1900: Zouave breeches, a check dress with royal blue trim, and a straw boater, her hands covered in the precious stones Doctor Mardrus had brought back from Ceylon. As one critic commented, "For 1900 style it would be hard to find better" (Billy 1951: 226).

Thus Lucie, at the age of twenty-six, having slept in her mother's room with her sister all the time the family lived in Paris, was married before she knew what was happening. She had not yet recovered from her three year passion for Impéria and trustingly told her husband the story of her infatuation, showing him a photograph she had of the woman. Joseph-Charles looked calmly at the picture, declared "she was beautiful," putting the affair firmly in the past tense, and tore the photo to pieces (Delarue-Mardrus 1938: 119). For him it was nothing but a boarding school romance, of no interest and no importance. In this his opinion was entirely conventional, for lesbian passions are frequently dismissed as merely a phase, even when, as in Lucie's case, they last a lifetime and survive the stormiest of romantic marriages. Lucie, however, knowing her own emotions better than her husband, was certain that she would never feel such heartache again in her life. "I no longer had a moment to think over my passion for Impéria" (Delarue-Mardrus 1938: 124), she reflects.

It was now her duty to set about getting to know and understand the man she had married, a hard task, for Joseph-Charles was a quick-tempered, unpredictable man with a love of the dramatic. He would stand naked in the doorway when the landlady came to collect the rent, and fell out with Guillaume Apollinaire over a cat he is reputed to have killed (Barney 1960: 155). In time Lucie did indeed come to understand him as no one else did, but she never seems to have felt for him the passion she reserved for women.

To give him his due, it must be said that it was Joseph-Charles who introduced Lucie to French literary society, her first poems being published in the *Revue Blanche* on which he collaborated, and it was to him more than to anyone else that she owed the success of her literary career. Though she had made friends of her own, Sully Prudhomme, Sirieyx de Villers, Hélène Vacaresco, Sarah Bernhardt, Edmond Rostand, Robert de Montesquiou, Marguerite Durand, and the editors of *La Fronde*—not a bad collection for a young poet—her poetry was not taken seriously until her husband, already the talk of Paris for his translations, presented her himself. At the age of twenty she had shown her poems to François Coppée, who spent a few seconds flicking through them, enquired whether it amused her to write poetry and then advised her to take up sewing instead. The wife of Joseph-Charles Mardrus was much harder to dismiss.

One of the new acquaintances Lucie's poetry brought her was the English lesbian poet Renée Vivien, whose poetry book she received one morning in the mail with a dedication full of praise for Lucie's poems. Lucie found a certain similarity between Renée's "sapphic volume" and the ones she herself had written for Impéria. Impulsively, she invited Renée to visit but was not particularly impressed, describing her as a blonde young woman with discouraged shoulders and brown eyes, negligently dressed. Renée's conversation was banal and her demeanour that of a rather ordinary British girl looking for a husband (Delarue-Mardrus 1938:143). Lucie was struck, however, by her heavy, delicate eyelids and her long black lashes, features which she was later to give to little Pierre, Aimée de Lagres's unwanted son in *The Angel and the Perverts*. She was much more impressed by Renée's friend, Evalina Palmer and her old-fashioned beauty—Evalina had striking red hair, which hung down to her feet and a face as pale as a Pre-Raphaelite angel.

It was in Evalina Palmer's box at the theatre that Lucie first met Natalie Clifford Barney. In her memoirs she states stoutly that Natalie was, is, and will remain one of her dearest friends (144), but before their relationship reached the firm ground of abiding friendship, Lucie was to go through yet another passionate bout of unrequited love with its associated pain, rage, and jealousy. Barney describes her first meeting with Lucie in unambiguously sexual terms, "Mme Mardrus was slim and quite tall in a princess gown which moulded her perfectly symmetrical figure. One felt that in the nude such a body would occasion no disappointment" (Barney 1960:147). Clearly from the first Barney was undressing Lucie with her eyes and feeling well-pleased with the result. For her part, Lucie was well-used to arousing feminine attention. Once more, she committed all that she could not say to verse in a series of poems, which she sent to Natalie and which Natalie published anonymously in 1957, twelve years after Lucie's death, as *Nos secrètes amours* (Our secret loves). The poems, written between 27 November 1902 and 27 August 1903, express Lucie's violent desire, Natalie's reluctance, and Renée's incorporeal presence even when Lucie and Natalie are alone together—perhaps the reason for Lucie's brusque dismissal of Renée's attractions and her championing of Eva Palmer.

Te vouloir, te vouloir! Et n'être qu'une femme
Sur le bord défendu de ta félicité
(To want you, to want you! And to be but a woman
On the forbidden edge of your happiness.)

Malgré la nuit de joie et les portes fermées
Je ne suis pas seule avec toi
Gomorrhe brûle autour de nous!
(Despite the night of joy and the closed doors
I am not alone with you
Gomorrha burns around us.)

Je t'attaquerai, je t'estropierai! Le bel et bref éclair que ferait une lame!
(I will attack you, I will cripple you! The fine short gleam of a knife's
    blade!)
(Plat 1994: 108−109)

The sharp-edged keenness of Lucie's desire for Natalie, her despair at finding Natalie still haunted by memories of Renée, and the desperate cry of frustration conveyed in these poems contrast starkly with those Lucie was writing to her husband at the same period. Her thoughts of him are expressed in sad, calm verses of childlike trust and sweetness.

Toi qui m'aimes, berce-moi contre toi
car voici qu'alanguie et toute morte de tendresse
mon âme amère s'y endort
comme un petit enfant sur le bras qui la porte. (Plat 1994: 111)
(You who love me, rock me against you
for here, languid and quite dead of tenderness
my bitter soul falls asleep)

Lucie looked upon men as friends and companions, accepted them as admirers, but kept her passion for women.

Natalie remarked that Lucie attracted just as many women as men around her, adding mischievously that several of Lucie's female admirers had not admired in vain. She continues with a list of women who kept company with Lucie at different times: Dora Stroiva with her guitar, Suzy Doyen and her sister, Edmée Daudet and Simone Chevalier who came to ask her advice on her first poems (Barney 1960: 168). Ironically, perhaps, Lucie devotes a page of her memoirs to the subject of young women who write love poems and send their passionate outpourings to the older women they adore (Delarue-Mardrus 1938: 107). Lucie describes such adoration as a damn nuisance (un embêtement). Earlier, recalling her careful upbringing on the family estate, Lucie has explained that even the phrase "je m'embête" (I'm bored) was considered bad form (70). Thus the use of the related term "embêtement" here emphasizes her impatience at being the cause of such youthful attractions. She throws the poems, unread, into the trash, or so she says. Natalie Barney, less concerned with bourgeois opinion, might have told a different story.

Joseph-Charles seems to have regarded his wife more as a priceless treasure than a sexual partner. His pet-name for her was the rather cold "la Princesse Amande," Princess Almond, because of her flawless white skin; hers for him was "le Calife Oeil," Caliph Eye, suggesting a certain fear of surveillance. Lucie believed that his sudden desire for her was "tout intellectuel" (entirely intellectual) and his odd request to Natalie Barney seems to bear this out.

Dear Blonde one, blonde whose flesh is like that of a banana, I shall put your friendship to the test. You recognize, as I do, the poetic genius of the Princess Almond and that she must save herself entirely for her work. I cannot, then, ask her to bear fruit of a different kind. Yet a child between us would be most welcome. Your friend, the Great Crab, believes that it would be a good division of labor if you who are idle, young and as healthy as one could wish for, if you would bear this child which I would beget with you with all the esteem and affection I owe you. (Barney 1960: 167)

Natalie apparently replied to this innocent proposition without rancor, explaining that while it was a most flattering proposal she could not do violence to her own nature even for a single occasion, or with such an important goal in mind. She and Lucie discussed the matter with great hilarity afterwards, preferring to see it as one of Joseph-Charles's little eccentricities and ignoring any more serious import it might have had.

The love of Lucie Delarue-Mardrus's later life was the Jewish opera singer, Germaine de Castro, whom she met on 17 November 1932, at the age of fifty-eight. It was Germaine's voice which captivated her. "Her voice, my drug, my morphine!" she would exclaim. In her memoirs she tries to explain what it was that attracted her to the singer,

her magnificent generosity; her unselfconscious courage; her tender sensitivity; the complete, almost stunning lack of small-mindedness . . . ; the scrupulous conscientiousness she brings to her work as an artist . . . ; her native sadness, offset by an invigorating gaiety, all this, even the crudeness of her speech and the brutality of her indomitable frankness whose barbs I have sometimes suffered. (Delarue-Mardrus 1938: 310)

Lucie's old friend, Myriam Harry, remembers how, once Lucie had met Germaine and heard her sing, the woman became "her only passion, her only reason for living." Harry adds wryly, "We hardly saw her any more. No one saw her" (Harry 1946: 124).

On the quality of Germaine's voice, opinions differ, but

there was such passionate antagonism to Lucie's new liaison that it is hard to believe any of the assessments of her friends and acquaintances were anything approaching objective. A Monsieur Imbert, writing in the *Journal des débats,* stated more coolly,

Madame Germaine de Castro's is not one of those voices which astound the listener by their volume, their range or the singularity of their tone. What she has is a pleasant, average organ, but what with consummate art she wields it, with what technical perfection she modulates its sonority. (Imbert in *Journal des débats,* 14 May 1930, quoted in Plat 1994: 212)

It seems, then, that Germaine's voice was superbly trained and imbued with a passionate intensity. Many singers nowadays who are idols of the public cannot boast of so much.

Lucie threw not only her heart and soul into her new love, but also all her time and most of her money. Germaine's career was very much on the wane when Lucie met her. She had just been turned down for a recording contract with Columbia, and her greatest claim to fame was that she was Marian Anderson's singing teacher. In order to relaunch Germaine in the public eye, Lucie organized a series of performances at prominent music halls in Paris, offering to accompany the singer herself, thereby lending her own name to the spectacle. Her friends and admirers, however, felt most strongly that the vulgarity of the music hall scene was beneath Lucie, fearing a loss of social status for her if she persisted. The Germaine-Lucie act, heralded by a melodramatic drum roll, and preceded by clowns and acrobats dressed in gaudy colors, was, it seems, too shocking to the delicate upper-class Parisian constitution. Harry remarks upon Germaine's entrance, "a big fat woman with a tragic face dressed all in black," and the thin pathetic figure of Lucie by her side, muffled up in shawls with spectacles on her nose, bent over the music (Harry 1946:125). Even Lucie's faithful servant, Berthe,[3] cried her way through the performance.

Natalie Clifford Barney herself watched the new developments with anxiety. Cushioned by the four million dollars provided by her father's railroad fortune (a sum which would be worth about one billion nowadays), she was both used to and amused by the disapproval and disapprobation of the small-minded bourgeoisie who professed themselves shocked by her extravagant lesbianism, as though at a breach in the good table manners which they themselves had only recently, and most painstakingly, learned. Lesbianism was an upper-class privilege and Germaine de Castro was distinctly vulgar. Barney might be a lover of women, but she talked like a lady. Germaine suffered also from the twin social faults of corpulence at a time when slimmer figures were the fashion—Renée Vivien, the love of Barney's life had, after all, died of anorexia—and that of being "no longer young." Lucie saluted Germaine's greater maturity in her novel, *Une Femme mûre et l'amour* (Love and the mature woman) but what Lucie calls "mûre" (ripe), Barney called "obese." In her portrait of Lucie, Barney confides that she tried to make her friend change her mind with regard to Germaine. The first performance of Germaine's that Lucie attended was called, "La Chanson à travers les âges" (Song through the ages). Maliciously Natalie warned Lucie, "Watch out lest 'Song Through the Ages' become 'Aging through Song'" (Barney 1960: 175). The following year, when Lucie announced her music-hall project, Natalie asked spitefully, "Haven't you taken a good look at your soprano?" pointing out how fat Germaine had grown.

Lucie's own sister, Charlotte, was quite used to Lucie's passionate affairs with women. Lucie's friend and neighbor, Chattie, had accompanied her on many of her speaking tours and Miss Trott, Chattie's successor, an American violin teacher, had been welcomed everywhere Lucie went. Yet Charlotte quarreled with Lucie violently about Germaine de Castro. "Catastrophe!" Lucie writes in her memoirs (309). "My sister greeted me with a frightful jealous fit, with the most offensive words for Germaine, the most shocking innuendoes about my trip to Le Havre, desperate, frightening, even vulgar." Lucie was forced to choose between Germaine and her friends and family. She picked Germaine and never spoke to Charlotte again. Many years later, after her sister's death when Lucie was in her late sixties, she suggested to her brother-in-law that she move in with him and they keep house together as friends and companions. The brother-in-law welcomed the proposal, but, in loyalty to his wife, laid down the condition that Lucie break off all contact with Germaine and not even mention her name. A condition that, naturally, she refused.

Lucie was not merely in love with a woman, again—from the age of six, after all, her most passionate relationships had been with women—but with a Jewish woman, who had a working-class "Parigot" accent and a decidedly vulgar way with words. That a working-class accent should be the cause of serious social ostracism may seem strange in the United States where the dollar standard makes plain a person's social position. In France, as in England, however, the way one spoke (or perhaps I should say "speaks" for in my experience this is still true today) marked one more clearly than the designer labels—or their lack—on one's clothes. Indeed, the upper classes of Europe are frequently more carelessly dressed than the middle class, their insouciance a badge of class. Homosexuality has always been a tolerated aristocratic idiosyncrasy, unless insistent attention is called to it. Of Delarue-Mardrus's most outspoken critics, Natalie Barney and Myriam Harry, the former would be the last to condemn Lucie for embarking upon a lesbian affair, and the latter was herself Jewish and so unlikely to disapprove for reasons of anti-Semitism. Lucie might list the crudeness of Germaine's speech among her greatest attractions, but then she was famous for her finely tuned ear and her ability to repeat and relish the language of others, from the colorful dialect of the Norman fishermen—reproduced in *Graine au vent* (Seed in the wind) and *L'Ex-voto,* to the Arabic cadences of the North African singers she met in Algiers and which she copied, almost perfectly, in her own singing.

The advent of the Second World War and the rise of anti-Semitism in France contributed strongly to Delarue-Mardrus's decline in popularity. As the thirties progressed, many prominent high society figures and friends of the author would make strongly anti-Semitic statements, including Gabriele D'Annunzio, who gave Mussolini the title of 'il duce' and Natalie Barney, who, though her maternal grandfather was Jewish, made Jewish people the butt of various aphorisms: "What nation will love the Jews so much that they may stop being Jewish?" (1910: 66); "A straightened Jewish nose: surgery, paraffin or mixed ancestry?" (1920: 129).

In 1940, Maurice Goudeket, Colette's husband, was arrested and sent to a camp in the south of France, to await deportation to Germany. Fortunately he was freed, thanks to the intervention of Colette's influential friends, and was hidden by a network of neighbors and shopkeepers in the Palais-Royal district of Paris for the rest of the war. His arrest nevertheless had a chilling effect on Colette's friends and Delarue-Mardrus feared for de Castro's life. Though her rheumatism was extremely painful and she longed to move south to a warmer climate, a move that was suggested to her by her sister, Suzanne, and that might have been expedited by the good offices of Maréchal Pétain, her youthful suitor, Delarue-Mardrus refused adamantly to leave de Castro. The couple, as well as de Castro's aged mother and the man de Castro had married to hide her Jewish identity, were then living in a house in Château-Gontier in Normandy.

One morning, as was inevitable, de Castro was called to the Kommandantur of the region and returned with a gold star on the back of her coat. In Autumn 1943, after the fall of Stalingrad, anti-Semitic persecution intensified. A friend of the de Castro household reported seeing an old Jewish teacher, who was paralyzed, being beaten with a club and thrown into the back of a truck. A gay friend of Delarue-Mardrus, the art collector, Chartrère, who was already hiding his Jewish lover, Sérézine, offered to let de Castro hide in another property he owned in a more remote area of the country. De Castro fled. The Gestapo came to the house, searched everything, interrogated the inhabitants, and threatened to take Delarue-Mardrus away if they could not find de Castro.

After *Fleurette* was banned by the Gestapo and her *Poèmes mignons* were withdrawn from the school curriculum, Delarue-Mardrus's subsequent poems and novels were each rejected in quick succession. Her *Souvenirs d'Orient* was returned to her by Plon as "insufficiently newsworthy to interest the public," which might be translated as meaning that they feared a liberal, even sentimental view of the Near East might be antipathetic to the Nazi censors at the time of their North African campaign. Many publishing houses lost their most valuable editors to anti-Semitism. Others were closed down and their property seized. Discouraged, Lucie put her rejected manuscripts away, baptizing them "Editions Dutiroir" (Bottom Drawer Press). Even her typist turned against her and returned her latest novel, *Etoile de David* (Star of David), refusing to type it "because it's too disrespectful to God the Father" (Harry 1946: 202). Lucie's rheumatism was by now so painful it was out of the question for her to type her work herself.

Worried about her failing health and frightening lack of money, friends in Paris tried to secure a pension for her. The tide did finally begin to turn. The Société des Gens de Lettres provided her with an income and sold the film rights to her novel *Graine au vent;* while *Souvenirs d'Orient* was bought by a publisher in Lyons. Whereas Delarue-Mardrus published four titles in 1938, three novels and an autobiography, she published barely one book a year thereafter. The Second World War marked the end of an era; after such a cataclysm nothing was to remain unchanged. As she had remarked in *Up to Date* (1936), "France remained aristocratic under three republics, and is now like a great lady of the manor

who married a wine merchant" (Newman-Gordon 1991:
110, her translation). Like the aristocratic France she cham-
pioned, Delarue-Mardrus did not survive the new alliance.

Part Two: The Harlequinade

The ambiguous silhouette of a figure with two faces can be seen prowling
at various carnivals in modern dress. The real bourgeoisie does not frequent these places, or rather what is left of the real bourgeoisie in a Paris
heading more and more toward a confusion of genders, a Paris in which
the society of the post war years is toppling the divisive barriers one
after another, leaving only an undifferentiated, multicolored mob, whose
numbers are increased by the surreptitious invasion of the foreigner, adding an extra intensity to the colors of this phrenetic harlequinade. *The
Angel and the Perverts, Intermezzo, 163*

When it first appeared in Paris in 1930, *The Angel and the
Perverts* was seen as little more than a *roman à clé* in which
the ambiguous two-faced silhouette who prowls its way
through a series of modern carnivals depicts Delarue-
Mardrus herself, the angelic, asexual outsider who observes
and reports on the immoral goings-on of Paris's sexual underworld, the main characters easily identifiable as friends
of hers or famous personalities of the time. Not only did
contemporary critics consider the novel a *roman à clé*, Delarue-Mardrus herself admitted in her memoirs "In *The
Angel and the Perverts* I analyzed and described Natalie
(Barney) at length as well as the life into which she initiated
me" (144), adding that she herself was not to abandon the
asexual role of the archangel until some time later. The
enraging, engaging, impassioned Laurette Wells is unques-
tionably the American writer and salon hostess, Natalie Clifford Barney (who also appears as Flossie in Liane de Pougy's

Idylle sapphique [Sapphic idyll] [1901] and Colette's *Claudine s'en va* [Claudine and Annie] [1903]; as Evangeline Musset in Djuna Barnes's *Ladies Almanack* [1928]; and as Valerie Seymour in Radclyffe Hall's *The Well of Loneliness* [1928]); the unfortunate Aimée de Lagres is a portrait (of sorts) of the English lesbian poet, Renée Vivien, one of Barney's most important lovers, though Barney was, in her understated way, highly offended by the portrait. "Renée pregnant! Only Lucie could have imagined such a thing. In reality, Lucie was jealous of Renée" (Chalon 1976: 210). The Countess de Talliard is, of course, the Baroness Hélène von Zuylen de Nyevelt, known as "la brioche" for her corpulent figure and round topknot of hair. (It was, incidentally, *brioche* not cake that Marie Antoinette suggested the peasants eat upon being told that they had no bread.) Other, less central characters are harder to place. The long-suffering but enamored Cecil Hampton must be Barney's ever-aspiring, ever-rejected beau, Manners-Sutton. The gay, opium-addicted, pajama-wearing Julien Midalge is, perhaps, Jean Lorrain, journalist and novelist of the Belle Epoque, real name, Paul Alexandre Martin Duval. Or maybe it's the dramatist Jean Cocteau, though he was not part of Lucie's social set and she does not mention him in her memoirs. But who is the Hanoum Iffet Effendi, the Turkish Princess who suddenly appears in Natalie's, sorry Laurette's, car as it heads for the Sarthe? Could she be Renée Vivien's old flame, Kérimé, the Turkish princess? And who, then, is Charlie, the reckless American flapper with her cigars, her almost shaven head, her masculine clothes, and her most unmanly terror of bulls?

These questions, with their insistence on the autobiographical interest of the novel, to the exclusion of its style and literary merit, act as a covert condemnation for the crime of frivolity. In these serious days *post mortem auctoris*[4] this is tantamount to damning the novel itself as not worth reading. Bernard Grasset, the publisher of a new biography of Lucie Delarue-Mardrus by Hélène Plat, publicized the book by putting a scarlet band around it announcing, "Sarah Bernhardt. Marcel Schwob. Gide. Octave Mirbeau. Jarry. Colette. Anna de Noailles. Natalie Barney. Maeterlinck. Rodin. Valéry. Isadora Duncan. Heredia. Félix Fénéon." And that's it. Just a list of names of 1920s luminaries. Clearly what interests the publisher about Delarue-Mardrus was who she knew. This vaunting of the author's social position and its corresponding neglect of her craft and skill is not unlike the instruction Gabrielle Réval suggested Delarue-Mardrus give her manager in 1924. Before embarking upon a lecture tour of the United States, she should whisper in his ear, "Don't tell the Americans that I am a famous woman in my own country, but that of all women poets I have most often been photographed" (Réval 1924: 55). Lucie Delarue-Mardrus was beautiful and she was well-connected, but these qualities alone cannot explain the success of her fiction.

The Angel and the Perverts is not merely a *roman à clé* but a novel of social turbulence, reflecting a time when fortunes had been lost and found, social boundaries were becoming more fluid, and gender roles were less restricting. Mario/Marion, the hermaphrodite hero/ine, is two-faced not only because of his/her ambiguous genitalia (gently alluded to rather than explicitly defined in the text), but also due to an ambiguous economic and social position. The family's fall from economic grace is described in far greater detail than the anatomy of the son/daughter and heir/ess. The child of a ruined aristocrat and a parvenue coal heiress, a French Catholic and an English Protestant, later forced to make a living as a legal secretary and hack writer (in female and male guises respectively), Marion benefited from, and in his/her own person represented, not only the "sexual confusion" of the times but also the social confusion which Delarue-Mardrus likens to a "phrenetic harlequinade." While she addressed the topic of homosexuality explicitly in only three of her books, the theme of bourgeois versus aristocratic values may be seen throughout her work. In *L'Ame aux trois visages* (1929), for example, the new wealth and ostentation of the mother, daughter of rich mill owners, is continually contrasted with the perfect taste and genteel poverty of the father's mother. *Hortensia dégénérée* (Withered hydrangea) tells the story of Count Ernoult de Beauvaisnes and the choice he must make between the daughter of a ruined French nobleman and an American heiress. After a brief affair with the former, he marries the latter. By the end of the story both the ruined noblewoman and the Count have drowned themselves in a pond where the Count had plucked a hydrangea and let it wither like the fortunes of the noble house.

Delarue-Mardrus was born at the beginning of the Belle Epoque, a time of great social upheaval in Paris with the humiliating defeat of the Franco-Prussian War (1870–1871), the ravages of the civil uprising in the Paris Commune (1871), the Siege of Paris (1877), the vast urban landscaping of Baron Haussmann with its consequent uprooting of many neighborhoods, the Dreyfus Affair of the 1890s, and the cataclysm of the First World War. The dynastic powers of the old guard aristocracy had been swept away with the disappearance of the *ancien régime* during the French Revolution of the previous century; now it was the *haute bourgeoisie* that found itself, and its entrenched status, under attack. Although the daughter of a shipping lawyer, who had rented rather than inherited the family home, and thus bourgeois herself, Delarue-Mardrus, with an upward identification typical of her class, thought of herself as part of the nobility she mixed with. In this she resembled the arch snob, Marcel Proust; they shared a taste in titled aristocracy, for both were close friends of Elisabeth de Gramont, Duchess of Clermont-Tonnerre and Robert de Montesquiou, on whom Proust's Charlus was based. When she pits the virtuous, understated aristocracy against the vulgarity of the bourgeoisie, it is the new distinction between *haute* and lower bourgeoisie that is really at issue.

Describing his/her stay at his/her uncle and aunt's house, Marion explains that it was the horrors s/he saw perpetrated in the name of bourgeois convention that gave him/her a taste for social outlaws. Indeed, in one telling passage in *The Angel and the Perverts,* Delarue-Mardrus makes plain her championing, through Marion, of the noble purity of homosexual lifestyles in contrast with the base, mercenary nature of bourgeois mores.

At Laurette or Midalge's house one talks art, music, even love with respect and ceremony. Beauty and money are never discussed in the same sentence. For dirty perverts they are decidedly clean-minded. (Chapter Five, 115)

This is in stark contrast with the heterosexual journalist who "like a traveling salesman on a spree" makes it his business to fondle the legs and arms of a group of actresses sitting on a sofa and imagines the salon of the famous lesbian Laurette Wells to be a house of ill repute.

It is Marion's decidedly bourgeois aunt and uncle who have their "nephew" examined by a doctor and his civil status changed to that of a girl, whereas his parents preferred to keep him in discreet ignorance of his physical peculiarity. Bourgeois, then, is this new need for legal/medical labels, where the aristocracy of old preferred to understand at half a word and remain silent. It was its homogeneous privilege to condone idiosyncrasy, while the more heterogeneous bourgeoisie required quantification in the absence of traditional, ancestral standards. The predominance of quantification to establish quality is a common phenomenon in newly diverse societies where the old accepted codes are unusable, since only a small number of people are familiar with them. It would seem, then, that the ultimately countable, and accountable, money standard, otherwise known as a capitalist economy, is necessary to any multicultural, sexually diverse community. Until the processes of acclimatization, acculturation, and assimilation erode the differences once more, and obsessive counting gives way to the mystification and ceremoniousness beloved of those nostalgic for the aristocratic order, a quality Delarue-Mardrus shared with Proust, who would, for example, give his address by describing his neighborhood, his house, the illuminations, "It is the only window on the Boulevard Haussmann in which there is still a light burning!" (Benjamin 1968: 207), anything but the street number, which would define it as part of the bourgeois quantification system.

The seven volumes (but who's counting?)[5] of Proust's *A la recherche du temps perdu* make a cult of this nostalgia, whereas *The Angel and the Perverts,* published in 1930 (eight years after Proust's death) ostensibly describes the period in which it was written: Paris of the twenties. Though the material details—Laurette's car, Midalge's pajamas (popularized by Gilbert and Sullivan's *Mikado*), Charlie's flapper haircut—are all perfect 1920s artifacts, the sensibility, the social web, hark back to an earlier time, the early 1900s, the years of Delarue-Mardrus's infatuation with Natalie Clifford Barney. Plat subtitled her biography of the author "Une Femme de lettres des années folles" (A woman of letters of the *Années Folles*—or the *1920s*) but Delarue-Mardrus's writing is more characteristic of the Belle Epoque, which represented the tastes and passions of her youth. The difference between the two periods may be summed up in the contrast between the juxtaposition of the elegant and the extraordinary typical of *art nouveau,* and the insistent geometrics of *art deco.* Delarue-Mardrus's preoccupation was not with form but with capturing a moment.

Laurette's house in Neuilly with its abundant park is clearly based on Barney's house in Neuilly, from which she and Delarue-Mardrus would issue forth on horseback, riding along the banks of the Seine to the amusement of the local lads who mistook Delarue-Mardrus, in her masculine-looking jodhpurs, for a young man. "He's as pretty as a woman!" they would yell in derision (Harry 1946: 31). Yet by the 1920s Barney had been living in the rue Jacob on the left bank for more than a decade. The contrast between the moderate comfort of Miss Hervin's apartment in the 16th arrondissement, on the right bank, and the drab seediness of Marion de Valdeclare's three rooms on the left bank would, by the 1920s, no longer have been so stark. While the left bank had always been the haunt of artists, writers, and actors, by the twenties it had become much more fashionable to frequent such a milieu. Renée Vivien's affair with the Baroness Van Zuylen de Nyeveldt dated from 1901, and Laurette relates many episodes in her attempt to regain Aimée—the serenade under her window, the flowers at her door—which Barney had performed in her mission to get Renée back. Both the Countess Talliard's servants: butler, footman, maid, and those of Laurette Wells: chambermaid, manservant, driver, are more reminiscent of the great houses women of their class maintained earlier in the century. The language of the novel, too, is slightly old-fashioned. Though Marion calls Laurette "un chic type" (a brick, a good chap), an expression which was all the rage in the twenties, the servants and little Pierre's peasant foster-mother still address Laurette in the third person. "Si mademoiselle veut monter?" (if Mademoiselle wants to go upstairs?) suggests the butler, as Marion is shown into Laurette's house in Neuilly. "Ces dames vont entrer chez nous" (these ladies are going to come in), says the wet-nurse, ushering Laurette and Marion into her cottage. Although not anachronistic, these stylistic traits mark the novel as somewhat old-fashioned, the milieu as aristocratic rather than bourgeois, just as Marion's Louis-Seize and Directoire furniture denote old-fashioned good taste rather than modernity.

Though modern criticism conceptualizes the Paris of the 1920s as the time of Man Ray, the surrealists, and the later Cubists with their intense interest in form, individual expression, and the solipsism of the psyche, these movements were part of the avant-garde rather than the mainstay of cultural production. Though they have come to symbolize the period, they no more represent it than the Beatniks represent America in the fifties and early sixties, a time when large numbers of Americans were at home imbibing the conservative family values of Beaver Cleaver.[6] The new artistic currents are referred to in *The Angel and the Perverts,* but always with an amused condescension as of something *infra dig.*[7] Simone Luvedier, Julien Midalge's friend who undergoes an epiphanic conversion to Catholicism and dismays Marion, the purist, by her vulgar ostentation, is a dadaist poet—the dadaist movement being a precursor of surrealism. The brilliant young medical student who examines little Pierre, breaks into the poems of Valéry and Mallarmé on the drive back to Paris; while Laurette and Marion go upstairs to powder their noses, he strikes up Debussy's *Arabesque* on Laurette's piano. Laurette's acerbic comment, "He doesn't play badly, that young man. But too naively infatuated with modernism. I fear he may be an indifferent snob" (Chapter Fifteen, 212), seems to convey the author's own opinion of the modernist endeavor. The description of Marion's physical make-up owes more to the androgynous Salomes of the nineteenth-century symbolist painter Gustave Moreau than to Picasso's decontextualized women composed of straight lines and acute triangulations. Though the American expatriate painter Romaine Brooks, long-term lover of Natalie Barney, is known for her almost monochrome portraits of thin, pale women with elongated bodies, her inspiration was explicitly symbolist rather than modernist.

The scene in which the doctor examines Marion and pronounces him a girl is interesting in what it reveals of the medical/legal discourse on sexual anomaly of the time, or rather what elements of that discourse have reached the popular understanding, for, as will be elaborated later, Delarue-Mardrus always worked on issues which had captured the popular imagination. The doctor decides that, despite what was written on Marion's birth certificate, it is better to classify him/her among the female sex. He does not, therefore, declare that Marion is a woman, but sees the problem as one of classification: of the various, contradictory gender attributes Marion's body displays, do they cluster more around the male or the female end of the spectrum? The doctor's tone is scientific, which Marion finds "worse than all the jeers of my classmates" because it is unanswerable and yet expects, enforces, compliance.[8] The new bourgeois knowledge is not to be disputed; there is no appeal against science. Throughout the text Marion protests against the terrible curse that has set him apart from his fellow man, set her apart from her fellow woman. Because her/his physical peculiarity is unique, never previously encountered, there is no name for it and thus it cannot be spoken of. As s/he wanders through Paris, a lonely outsider, "alone of his/her kind," s/he is unable to do more than watch and witness the carnival of life, without joining in the revelry. Yet the doctor, upon examining his/her body, recognizes the problem immediately and is able to make comparisons with other cases of the same nature.

Unfortunate individuals like yourself are sometimes lucky enough to grow a beard, you understand. But yours will never grow and that will, in the end, excite suspicion. So it is best to make up your mind while there is still time. You are only nineteen years old, you are not yet known in the world. Cases like yours are not unheard of in the legal domain. It will be easy to have your status rectified at the next meeting of the medical board. (Chapter Four, 100)

Not only is Marion's case not unique, there appear to be gradations of symptoms: Some patients are able to grow beards, others not. The doctor can tell where on the spectrum Marion stands since her/his beard will never grow.[9] At this point, having outlined the relevant physical information (Marion's chronic beardlessness), and taking into consideration the appropriate details of social status (Marion is young and unknown), the doctor seems to hand the problem back to Marion, "it is best to make up your mind while there is still time." Apparently Marion is to be accorded the power to decide what sexual identification best suits him/her—a radical attitude to gender identity that even the hyper-individualist 1990s would be hard put to equal. But, as it turns out, this is a strategy to gain Marion's ideological obedience to a decision that is to be passed on to another authority: the law. The French verb "se décider" (to make up one's mind) can also convey the connotation of "to put a brave face on," "to set oneself to doing what one has to do anyway," and it is in this ambiguity of agency that the finesse of the doctor's speech rests. This difference in ideology, and the institutional apparatus backing up the ideology, represents the distinction between the old aristocratic *(haut bourgeois)* order and the now entrenched bourgeoisie. Where the old order ruled by inherited right, the bourgeoisie needs to gain the consent of its constituents, a much respected part of the democratic process. Consent requires information and thus at least the appearance of freedom and equality—two other touchstones of democracy. And it is the democratization of France that Delarue-Mardrus both abhors in her novels and profits from in her private life, for it allowed her to divorce her husband and live with the women she loved on the proceeds of her writing.

The doctor takes Marion through the necessary stages of entry into the bourgeois order: information, consent, legal approval, and referral to the proper authorities composed of pre-established experts. The appeal to legal discourse is interesting, confirming as it does the two-pronged assault of medical and legal authority, in opposition to the power of church doctrine, so prominent under the old order, and so influential on Marion's desolate childhood. Faced with their pupil's aberrant intellectual nature, the conclusion of the religious authorities, as represented by Marion's procession of *abbés,* is the cry of dismay, "He will become a Benedictine." The church provides a place for misfits, and though both the *abbés* and Marion's parents start up a coercing chorus of "to the Seminary!" s/he is able to leave that institution possessed of the degrees and qualifications that will later enable him/her to live an independent life in Paris's sexual underworld. The Jesuits do not throw him/her out, despite his/her physical peculiarity, nor do they believe it within their remit to alter his/her status. They merely inform his/her uncle—though of what, exactly, the reader is not told.

Not only are cases such as Marion's familiar to the doctor, but they are known in legal circles, too. This information is meant to be comforting. At last Marion has found someone to whom s/he is not unique, yet the medico-legal knowledge causes the change of civil status, which s/he thinks of as "the ultimate offense." The *abbés* of her/his childhood were not allowed to see his/her body, or express an opinion as to her/his sexual status. They merely categorize Marion's worrying intellectual prowess as "Benedictine." What is missing from the scene of the doctor's examination is any appeal to the new psychoanalytical knowledge. Freud had, after all, published his *Beyond the Pleasure Principle* in 1921, and the case of Dora dates from 1905. The reason for this is twofold. First, as discussed above, although published in 1930 when Delarue-Mardrus was fifty-six, the novel continually harks back to the Belle Epoque of the author's youth, a time when the new science of psychology was only in its infancy. Secondly, the author is at pains to avoid a psychological reading of Marion's torment by relating it continually to his/her physical condition.

The modern critics Pauline Newman-Gordon and Hélène Plat, identifying Marion closely with Delarue-Mardrus herself, see him/her as an androgynous-looking woman who cannot decide between the sexes. Newman-Gordon, in her brief biography of Delarue-Mardrus, considers the writer to have been ahead of her time in her depiction of sexual marginality. Although the subject of hermaphrodites has been a long-lived theme in French literature from Rabelais onward, in *The Angel and the Perverts,* Newman-Gordon notes, "an entire milieu comes alive" (1991 : 115). What is interesting about this assessment is the interpretation it gives, although not explicitly, of the meaning of Marion's hermaphroditism. Delarue-Mardrus does not, after all, describe a milieu of hermaphrodites but of lesbians and gay men. The physical facts of hermaphroditism—the possession of both male and female primary sexual organs—are seen as a metaphor for a bisexual libido. Indeed, Newman-Gordon calls the hero/ine of *The Angel and the Perverts* "the bisexual Marion," referring to him/her continually as "she." Yet

Delarue-Mardrus is at pains to make clear, in her charmingly guarded, neo-Victorian way, that for Marion anatomy is destiny, condemning him/her to a life outside of human sexuality, rather than facilitating the enjoyment of both male and female love objects. For Plat, Marion is an "androgynous angel," not a hermaphrodite, and thus bears a close physical similarity to Delarue-Mardrus herself, who, with her tall stature, slim hips, and small bust, was frequently described as androgynous. The sculptor, Rodin, for example, was eager to sculpt her body with its "Appollonian legs like those of a hermaphrodite" (Harry 1946: 34). Neither Newman-Gordon nor Plat comes to grips with the actual description of Marion in the novel; both critics ignore the important difference between androgyny and hermaphroditism. In modern parlance, the former is a popular and flattering term to describe the physical appearance of an, almost invariably, young adult who, if female, is tall, slim-hipped, and flat-chested, and, if male, beardless and delicate of limb, whereas the latter is a worrying medical diagnosis of anatomic and possibly (depending on the level of scientific knowledge) hormonal intersexuality. The first, based only on appearance, is a fashion judgment; the second, based on the biological facts of the body, is an expert condemnation. Delarue-Mardrus obstinately sets Marion's problem as an anatomical, not a psychological one: born with the genital organs of both sexes, but with no reproductive capacity, s/he is unable to have sexual feelings for either sex. Hers/his is a natural calamity, which must be endured patiently since it cannot be cured. There is something of the modern, conservative appeal to a "gay gene" as the origin of homosexuality here; a palliative offered to the religious right: we are all part of

God's mysterious plan, or at least part of nature. No desire, no free agency is to sow chaos in the smoothly dualistic sexual realm.

As Newman-Gordon rightly observed, the theme of hermaphroditism has constantly recurred in French literature. Before the modern medicalization of the body, however, it was either considered a curse of heaven, or used as a metaphor for wholeness or omniscience. Most authors were familiar with the classical accounts of hermaphroditism in Plato's *Symposium* and Ovid's *Metamorphoses*. In the *Symposium*, Aristophanes describes the original human as a double being with two male, two female, or a male and a female part. This being was later sundered by the gods and condemned to spend the rest of its life looking for its other half. Ovid tells the story of Salmacis, the water nymph who embraces the hapless Hermaphroditus, so named because he resembled both his father, Hermes, and his mother, Aphrodite. Hermaphroditus would not give in to Salmacis's charms, but she refused to let go of him, and so their two bodies were merged for all eternity. Instead of the perfection of the whole, however, Hermaphroditus has been unmanned by the merger. In the sixteenth century, Rabelais played on the idea of the hermaphrodite as a more complete person and describes a medallion on which has been struck the image of a two headed figure, but upon closer inspection it is clear that the two heads face each other, whereas in the classical hermaphrodite they would be looking in opposite directions. A little Renaissance joke for a copulating, heterosexual couple, or "two-humped beast." Thus the hermaphrodite may represent either heterosexual sex or homosexual desire.

In 1978, Michel Foucault published the memoirs of Herculine Barbin, a French hermaphrodite whose account of her/his life was discovered beside her/his dead body at his/her death in 1868. Herculine's life was, in some ways, the reverse of Marion's, and while it is improbable that Delarue-Mardrus had read the memoirs themselves, she will certainly have seen the accounts of hermaphrodites written by early twentieth-century sexologists like Magnus Hirschfield, which were popular in Paris in the twenties. Where Marion grew up as a boy and attended the all-male Jesuit seminary, Herculine grew up as a girl and inhabited the all-female worlds of a girls' orphanage, a convent, and a girls' school. Herculine's civil status was changed to that of a man in early adulthood, while Marion's was changed to that of a woman at about the same age. Herculine's autobiography alternates between the use of masculine and feminine pronouns and concord in ways that are similar to the gender alternation in *The Angel and the Perverts*. Both Herculine and Marion spend their childhoods in environments protected by religious authorities, only to have their secret despoiled by the medico-legal institution and the course of their lives irrecoverably altered. For each, sexual and genital anomaly are closely linked.

The hermaphrodite as metaphor for a perfect being was an important theme in the work of two contemporaries of Delarue-Mardrus and may have served as further inspiration. In *The Amazon and the Page* (1988:99–106) Karla Jay traces the theme of the hermaphrodite in the writings of Natalie Barney and Renée Vivien, from the portrait of San Giovanni in Vivien's *A Woman Appeared to Me* (1904b), who is sexless and immortal, to A.D. in Barney's *The One Who Is Legion, or A.D.'s Afterlife*, published in 1930, the same year as *The*

Angel and the Perverts. Where Marion is possessed of both genders, A.D. is genderless, though these descriptions may have been strongly influenced by the limitations and exigencies of the languages in which each text was written. For, unlike almost all her other work, Barney wrote *A.D.* in English, which, in the first person, requires no gender marking, while *The Angel and the Perverts* was written in French, where gender marking is obligatory. Like Marion, A.D. is asexual and therefore free to enter into the imagination and emotional lives of others without the fetters of sexual urges.

Though Delarue-Mardrus provides no foreword or introduction to the novel itself, some of her ideas about homosexuality and hermaphroditism can be seen in "Fable, Vérité" (Fable, truth), the first section of *Les Amours d'Oscar Wilde,* which serves as a prelude to her account of Wilde's life. Delarue-Mardrus begins by summarizing Aristophanes' speech from the *Symposium*. It reads like a classic introduction to the theme of the invert who is homosexual because originally derived from a male-male, or female-female, couple and who will inevitably be unhappy if not permitted to seek a mate of the same sex. However, Plato's hermaphrodite is only the first of a gallery of strange creatures presented in this section. Which are "fable," which "truth," is never clarified. The second vignette describes the friend of a well-known actress (who told Delarue-Mardrus the story herself, so it must be true). He was a Russian diplomat who was married but had "particular tastes" (i.e., he was gay). One day, Delarue-Mardrus recounts, the diplomat was knocked over by a car and needed an operation. Upon opening his abdomen, the surgeon was astonished to discover a complete set of female sex organs, revealing the man to be a hermaphrodite. The third section introduces us to various monsters, such as the Norman peasant woman who gives birth to a child with a calf's head, having been chased by a wild bull when pregnant. Delarue-Mardrus informs us sagely that the man is not the only factor in procreation; strong fear, a yearning for particular foodstuffs, and even repetitive dreams and obsessive thoughts in the mother may affect the baby. Why, Oscar Wilde's own mother stubbornly believed throughout her pregnancy that she would have a daughter. When the baby turned out to be a boy, she dressed him as a girl and let his hair grow, and look how he turned out. Homosexuality is, it seems, only one of nature's manifestations, somewhere between the pederast, the calf-headed child, the dog-man, the bearded lady, and the hermaphrodite. The portrayal of Marion in *The Angel and the Perverts* often echoes themes found in the classical stories of hermaphrodites, though the word "hermaphrodite" is used only once in the whole novel.

If Marion's mother accomplished a *tour de force* in helping Marion through childhood and adolescence without anyone knowing, not even him/herself, what an unusual creature s/he was, Delarue-Mardrus has accomplished another in her revelation/nonrevelation of Marion's physical peculiarity. On the first page the reader is told that Marion's mother must have been expecting twins when she was carrying him, for Marion has a strange second self. Thus from the first we know there is some mystery surrounding Marion, and our curiosity is stoked as to what the mystery might be. At first we share this curiosity with the young boy, who becomes our mouthpiece in the text. "I can't very well send you to the Jesuits," announces his father, to which Marion responds, as

we do, "Why?" We share his frustration at the nonrevelation
"Because." At the beginning of Chapter Two, however, we
are on our own. Who is this "she" who suddenly appears
in the novel, occupying Marion's place? It is only by the
characteristics she shares with Marion—the multi-hued blue
eyes, the hoarse voice and breaking laugh—that we begin to
recognize her. When Janine mocks Marion's antiemotional
stance, "What a pity! A beautiful young lady like you!"
Marion replies "Who said I was a young lady?" Now it is
her turn to tantalize the reader, as well as the textual ad-
dressee. There are three possible interpretations for this re-
mark, each of which gives it a different slant, based on age,
class, and gender respectively. The first interpretation is that
Marion is older than she seems and is therefore asserting her
maturity: not a young girl but an already established lady in
her thirties. The second is that Marion is not a young lady
but a woman, an important class distinction. Since she is
obliged to earn her own living and cannot afford even a maid
but has her concierge cook her meals, this interpretation has
some validity. The third possibility is, of course, that Marion
is a man, which Delarue-Mardrus is careful never to state
explicitly. Instead Marion is described as though she were
performing a role in a play. Thus, in Chapter Three, the
description "fille de trente ans" (girl of thirty) is appended to
Marion's name without a connecting verb, as though it were
an adjective describing the Marion of the moment. In the
next clause, "elle redevint l'éphèbe éternel qu'elle était" (she
became again the eternal youth she was). At a superficial
reading this suggests the author is finally divulging that Marion was really a boy. Yet the pronoun *elle* (she) militates
against this reading, had Marion been purely and simply a

boy, the pronoun *il* (he) would have been used: "he became again the eternal youth he really was." Instead a contradiction remains between the gender of the pronoun and that of the noun, reflecting the eternal contradiction of Marion's state.

Throughout the text the reader is tantalized with an almost unveiling of Marion's body. In Chapter Four, in which all is explained, the reader learns of "the nameless horrors" of Marion's childhood, the "unprecedent drama" of his/her birth, and the "masterpiece of deception" of his/her birth registration. When he sends him/her to the seminary, Marion's father, we are told, could easily imagine the methods his/her companions used to show him/her what a phenomenon s/he was; the director of the seminary "notifies" Marion's aunt and uncle—of what, the reader is not told. Later, to distract Laurette from her misery, Marion contemplates telling her his/her "real story." Yet no explicit word is given to the reader. Instead a double description is provided, one which skillfully manipulates the gender resources of the French language. Marion is both "seul" and "seule"—the masculine and feminine spellings of the adjective "alone"; s/he contemplates a future as either a "bénédictin" or "bénédictine" (male or female Benedictine); his/her imagination is both "mâle et femelle" (male and female). The leather-bound books that line the walls of Marion's bedroom are described as the pipes of a church organ (Chapter Twelve, 181), a metaphor that reinforces the monkish image of Marion's religious retreat, yet the French term "les orgues" is, as far as gender is concerned, one of the most intriguing and ambiguous in the French language. In the singular the word is masculine, while in the plural it becomes feminine. When referring to a church organ, although the referent is singular, the term becomes grammatically plural, requiring plural concord. A complicated piece of artillery, composed of many muskets, or, later, rockets, is also called "une grande orgue," thus the books are part of Marion's artillery in his/her personal gender battle.

The context in which the revelatory term "hermaphrodite" occurs is telling. "It amuses me to watch women in Paris who behave like men and men who behave like women. To me there is no more ridiculous sight than a false hermaphrodite," Marion declares with exasperation, upon being asked why s/he socializes with gay men and lesbians (Chapter Three, 89). A woman who behaves like a man, then, is one who is sexually attracted to women, making heterosexual attraction the defining factor of masculinity and femininity. An attraction to a person of the same sex as oneself is the property of the hermaphrodite who, whatever her/his sexual orientation, will always have one set of genitals in common with the object of his/her affections. Thus homosexuality is only authentic when biologically based. Yet Marion, our authentic hermaphrodite, repeatedly declares her/himself incapable of sexual attraction precisely because of his/her dual nature. "I love no one and nothing" is his/her catchword. S/he criticizes herself/himself for rebelling against Laurette's impropriety with the reflection "What was I to reproach others for their sexual fantasies, I who had no sex?" (Chapter Nine, 148).

The inauthenticity of homosexual behavior is underlined by the use of the French verb "faire," whose basic meaning is "to do" or "to make." Marion is amused by "des femmes qui font les hommes et des hommes qui font les femmes" (women who do—make, perform, act like—men and men who do—make, perform, act like—women). Masculinity and femininity are thus seen as active performances rather than passive states.[10] When Laurette is flirting with Marion, the hermaphrodite responds, "It's amusing when you play the lady's man. Especially with me. It's funny" (Chapter Two, 80). Again, it is the verb "faire" that is used to convey the sense of "playing" a lady's man. Masculinity is an act, a role. We hear later that Charlie, for all her mannish breeches, her authoritative swagger, and her short hair, is afraid of cows. Laurette informs the assembled company that when women dress (se déguisent) like men they always turn out to be sissies. "In every regard," she adds, in case the sexual nuance had slipped anyone's attention (Chapter Ten, 171).

If homosexuality is an inauthentic performance of cross gender roles, the text offers no prettier images of heterosexual men and women. Authenticity is not necessarily either natural or captivating. Marion's aunt and uncle are the epitome of bourgeois conventionality with their ostentatious furs and jewelry, which Marion ceremoniously despoils to reveal the emptiness beneath. Instead it is the pervert, Laurette, who suggests a route to Marion's salvation, a social function that will provide her with a stable, monosexual identity. In humorous exasperation, Laurette exclaims, "The search for paternity is a fine thing! A most unexpected . . . and most vexing method of playing the man!" (C'est beau la recherche de la paternité! Une façon bien inattendue . . . et bien embêtante de faire l'homme) (Chapter Fourteen, 203). Once more, the French verb "faire" suggests the active process of constructing a gender identity. Marion will adopt the unwanted child, become a mother, and consequently a woman. In the child's eyes, Marion will exist only as his mother, and this, Marion muses happily, "will give me a sex at last" (Chapter Fifteen, 215). The possibility of becoming a Benedictine, held out to Marion since childhood, still entails a certain ambiguity, for Marion might be either a monk or a nun. Instead of the contemplative life of the cloister, she chooses the secular service of motherhood, but either choice would entail a vow of celibacy, for the maternal role replaces the sexual role.

Marion constantly describes her/himself as a being alone, doomed to solitude for eternity, an observer who can never participate, but who, paradoxically, knows life from all angles. In this s/he is the epitome of the Belle Epoque "flâneur," or stroller, who walks the boulevards of Haussmann's new Paris, as well as the less frequented alleys of the capital, commenting on the scenes s/he witnesses but of which s/he is not part. Thus while Marion might be a creature apart in this novel, if one takes a quick intertextual glance at the novels and poems that preceded its publication, it is apparent that s/he was accompanied in her/his nocturnal wanderings by a ghostly horde of nineteenth-century literary figures from Baudelaire and de Nerval's dispossessed, or otherwise disgruntled, young men—the former splenetic, the latter morose—to Lautréamont's demonic Maldoror. Though Marion complained of being sterile (an egg with a clear yolk), her/his literary antecedents and successors are legion. At his/her darkest hour, wandering aimlessly along the banks of the Seine in the pouring rain, Marion's despairing bleat, "My heart was sucked by the leeches of despair" (Mon coeur était sucé par la ventouse du désespoir) (Chapter Nine, 143), is pure Baudelaire, one of the most popular French poets of all time. One is never alone when quoting Baudelaire.

Though Plat found the depiction of homosexuality in *The Angel* rather risqué for the period, and Newman-Gordon sees Delarue-Mardrus as ahead of her time in her depiction of sexual marginality, the late twenties and early thirties witnessed a veritable blossoming of novels on the subject. Indeed the publication of *The Angel* came hot upon that of Radclyffe Hall's *The Well of Loneliness* (1928), Virginia Woolf's *Orlando* (1928), and Delarue-Mardrus's own biography, *Oscar Wilde's Love Affairs* (1929). The way had been paved by the success of the lesbian works of the 1880s and early 1900s. Rachilde's *La Marquise de Sade* had been published in 1887, her *Madame Adonis* in 1888, followed by *Monsieur Vénus* in 1902. *Idylle sapphique,* by Liane de Pougy, which recounts the affair between the author, a Parisian courtesan, and the seventeen-year-old Natalie Barney, was published in 1901; Barney's *Cinq Petits Dialogues grecs,* inspired by her reading of Sappho's poetry, appeared in 1902. Renée Vivien's *Une Femme m'apparut,* a romantic fictionalization of her relationship with Barney, came out in 1904, as well as *La Dame à la louve,* a collection of short stories, which includes a lesbian retelling of the tale of Prince Charming. Lucie Delarue-Mardrus knew each of these authors personally (with the probable exception of Virginia Woolf), for Radclyffe Hall, Rachilde, and Liane de Pougy all frequented Barney's literary salon.

Liane de Pougy remarks that in *Idylle sapphique,* her account of the consequences of the vice (of lesbianism) is quite damning and explains "I wanted to express myself particularly severely on that point. This was actually quite important in order to find a publisher willing to publish a book on the subject at the time when my novel appeared," she recalls (Pougy 1977: 280). And yet the novel describes the central lesbian relationship as a haven from the brutality and greed of men. The male customers of the Parisian courtesan, Annhine de Lys, are described as "very rich and very ordinary" (Pougy 1979: 92). They bark unpleasantly aggressive orders like "Take your clothes off!" (123), "Naked . . . Completely naked!" (ibid.: 124), while the adoring young Flossie, on the other hand, smiles sweetly, murmuring romantically, "Let us unite our lips" to which Annhine responds, "I feel different. You let me glimpse so many things I never knew existed" (78). As its title suggests, the novel is an "idyll," despite the lacing of critical commentary. In contrast to the opinions of Plat and Newman-Gordon outlined above, I would suggest that in her rather guarded depiction of the lesbian and gay social milieux of Paris, far from being risqué, Delarue-Mardrus was perhaps more conservative than necessary. Colette had already gotten away with sensuous descriptions of sex between women in her Claudine series, especially in *Claudine en ménage* (Claudine married) (though these were, admittedly, organized for the delectation of the male gaze), whereas Delarue-Mardrus permits the reader only a voyeuristic frisson at the thought that if Marion's physical state were known, one lifetime would not suffice to cultivate all his/her perversity, before the possibility is closed off, Marion defined as "only a brain" and the whole idea dismissed in Marion's "horror of physical coupling" (Chapter Four, 98).

According to Plat, Marion's ambiguous sexuality is due to Delarue-Mardrus's own desire to compete with Colette's more sexually provocative style, but the homosexual milieu is not one in which she feels comfortable, and so the attempt falls flat (Plat 1994: 204). Newman-Gordon reinforces Plat's opinion, stating that Delarue-Mardrus is describing "a way of life which for a short time she had adopted" (Newman-Gordon 1991: 115). But the homosexual haunts of Paris were as familiar to Delarue-Mardrus as they were to Colette. If Colette's affair with "Missy," Mathilde de Morny, also known as the Marquise de Belboeuf, daughter of the Duke of Morny, was well-known, so too was that of Delarue-Mardrus and Natalie Barney. Delarue-Mardrus never remarried after her divorce from Joseph-Charles, but for the rest of her life enjoyed a series of long-term affairs with women, whereas Colette married three times and each time with passion—quite a testament to the appeal of heterosexuality. One of the characters Colette describes in *Le Pur et l'impur* (first published as *Ces Plaisirs* [These pleasures]) is Renée Vivien, an old friend and admirer of Delarue-Mardrus. *The Angel and the Perverts,* with its frequent movement between the lesbian literary salon, the gay soirée and the theatrical "bearpit," shows some fleeting resemblance to Colette's *Ces Plaisirs.* But the former is a novel, the latter presented as a nonfiction report and it was not published until 1932, two years after Delarue-Mardrus's novel. Nor was the theme of homosexuality entirely new to Delarue-Mardrus; she had addressed the topic the previous year in *Les Amours d'Oscar Wilde* (1929), as well as in *Sapho désespérée* (Sappho in despair) (an unpublished verse play, circa 1917, performed at the Théâtre Fémina under the ironic reversal "Phaon victorious"). Delarue-Mardrus was a personal friend of Lord Alfred Douglas, Wilde's lover, and it was her friendship for

Douglas that inspired her to write the biography. Despite these well-known autobiographical details, Delarue-Mardrus has often been cast as an outsider to lesbian and gay lifestyles, both by the critics of the day and by those of our own time. Even Barney reinforces this image in her portrait of Delarue-Mardrus (Barney 1960: 147–186), insisting as she does on describing Lucie and her husband, the infamous Joseph-Charles, as though her husband had been the most important person in Lucie's life.

It is true that Delarue-Mardrus felt a strong rivalry with Colette, to whom she was frequently compared. Indeed, *Le Petit Parisien* was to reject one of her novels, suggesting she write more "in Colette's style" (Plat 1994: 249). Delarue-Mardrus was in the habit of writing to Colette after a new book came out to correct her grammar and comment on her style. "You're jolly proud of yourself, now, having managed to squeeze the word 'anatiferous' into your latest book to astound us all. Well, I'm very sorry to have to inform you, but one should say 'invectiver contre' (to rail against) and 'tâcher à' (to try to)" (Plat 1994 : 276). Colette, apparently, took Lucie's chiding in good part. After her friend's death, she was to miss her little homilies. "I wish she were still amongst us, busy scolding me. I thought of her when I wrote the word 'photade.' She would have reproached me for it in her childish voice" (Plat 1994: 277). It was a sore point with Lucie, too, that Colette, the Burgundian, who had scarcely ever left her native France and spoke only French, was invited to christen *La Normandie,* the largest ferry boat in the world, as representative of *Le Journal,* while Lucie, who had written for this paper for years, came from Normandy, spoke fluent English, and had traveled widely, got passed over (Plat

1994 : 224). Perhaps the key to Colette's increasing success as the century advanced, as well as to Delarue-Mardrus's decrease in popularity, may be seen in Liane de Pougy's assessment of Colette. In her memoirs, *My Blue Notebooks,* de Pougy expresses a stern disapproval of Colette's novels, writing of *Chéri* that "every detail reveals its vulgarity." Though she professes admiration for Renée Vivien, Anna de Noailles, and Lucie Delarue-Mardrus, among other women writers of the period, she criticizes Colette for appealing to the reader's latent sensuality, tickling their sex, shaking up their kidneys, and going to their heads (Pougy 1977: 124–125). It seems that where Colette kept apace with, and was even influential in forming, public taste, Delarue-Mardrus's old-fashioned reserve held her back. Another of her editors begged Delarue-Mardrus to give him "a society tea," advising her to stop harping on about fairies, skeletons, mermaids, and archangels, tastes of a bygone age reminiscent of Edgar Allan Poe, Baudelaire, and the children's books of the *Bibliothèque rose*. It was, in part, Colette's very "vulgarity" that kept her in the public eye at a time when the old definitions of who, exactly, that public included were being burst apart. The launch of the *Normandie* represented not only Colette's success, but also the massive increase in adult leisure time that had contributed to it.

Though she was somewhat eclipsed by Colette's success in later years, at the height of her career Delarue-Mardrus was contributing to all the major papers in Paris and publishing not one but several novels a year. She considered herself first and foremost a poet, but she was also one of the most highly paid women fiction writers of her day. In 1914, at the beginning of the First World War, she took a post as a nursing auxiliary in the hospital in Honfleur as part of the war effort, just as Radclyffe Hall was driving ambulances in Paris. Hearing that the hospital desperately needed an X-ray machine, she bought one from the money she earned for one article in the *Journal*. Since X-ray machines cost a considerable sum, then as now, this fact alone bears witness to Delarue-Mardrus's spectacular popularity.

Her early success as a novelist was, in part, due to her extraordinarily acute ear for what would appeal to the contemporary imagination. Most of her novels were serialized in Parisian journals before being published as complete books, and they enjoyed some of the elements of the cliff-hanger: dramatic events that would not be resolved until the next chapter, sudden changes of character, place, and point of view. As the story unfolded week by week the novel characters were imbued with something of the immediacy of real life personalities.

With Joseph-Charles, Lucie traveled widely in North Africa and the Middle East, for a period of about seven years, sometimes being away for as much as a year at a time. The editor of the *Journal*, Catulle Mendès, suggested she write articles on her travels, which were then illustrated with daring pictures of the young woman on camelback, in front of the Sphinx in Egypt, or riding astride Arabian horses in the Sahara. Where Gide's adventures in North Africa were shocking, adult reading, Lucie Delarue-Mardrus introduced French readers to the more respectable exoticism of the married couple. Left by her husband in a Turkish harem while he went off on other business, Lucie would report on the pretty customs, the silks, the silver dishes, and the oriental singing of the women. These accounts were so successful that she was soon asked for a novel and it was in this way that her writing career had begun. As a professional writer, living entirely on the proceeds of her novels and lecture tours, Delarue-Mardrus was obliged to keep an eye on the enthusiasms of her fellow citizens. Thus in 1916 she published the novel *Un Roman civil en 1914* (A civilian novel in 1914), which, in a fervor of patriotism, tells the story of a young soldier and his sweetheart at the beginning of the First World War.

Early in the century, linguistics, with its rigorous analysis of language, began to make itself felt in the form of romance dialectology. With the first reports of Gilliéron's dialect dictionary of France, a project that was carried out from 1903–1909, the preservation and recording of the minority languages and dialects of France came to be seen as a fascinating and worthwhile endeavor. This awakening interest can be seen in two of Delarue-Mardrus's most successful novels, *L'Ex-voto* (made into a film entitled *Diable au coeur*) and *Graine au vent* (of which a film adaptation appeared in 1943, directed by Maurice Gleize), in which the dialect of the Norman peasants and fishermen are depicted in a series of dramatic episodes. Observing the success of her husband's translation of the *Thousand and One Nights,* as well as the popularity of her own articles about her travels through Algeria, Egypt, the Lebanon, Saudi Arabia, the Crimea, and Turkey, Lucie promptly polished off several novels with middle-eastern themes, including *L'Amanit* and *El Arab.*

Her first novel, *Marie, fille-mère,* telling the sad story of an unwed mother, appeared every Friday in the *Journal.* Many bourgeois readers professed themselves scandalized and stopped their subscriptions, while many others began to

buy the paper in order to read about Marie Avenel, raped by
le fils Budin while still only an innocent young girl, giving
birth to her son, Alexandre, forced to leave her village in
Normandy because of the social stigma. It was a shocking
and timely novel, reflecting and questioning the position of
women in the early 1900s. For Marie is "a creature defense-
less against the physiological fatality which holds women
down" (1908: 356). She dies, as she has lived, a victim of
masculine desire, for her young son is killed by her husband
in a fit of jealous rage and poor Marie Avenel's heart gives
out. Lucie is explicit about the cause of Marie's misfortunes.
"A man had committed the crime of forcing a child upon
her, another man had committed the crime of killing that
child. Marie's whole life was encompassed by the two acts"
(356). The novel was based, loosely, on the misadventures of
Lucie's own maid, transported to a country setting, with
extra realism added after a month spent in a labor ward
doing research in the guise of a medical student. One of
the women in the labor ward, who was dying from the
complications of a difficult birth, recognized Lucie and told
her she was an avid reader of *Marie, fille-mère*, and the
continuing series was being put aside for her to read as soon
as she was better. Unfortunately she died the following day.
Le Roman de six petites filles (Delarue-Mardrus's second
novel) tells the story of the pretty young English governess,
Miss Olive, her affair with the man of the house, and her
subsequent disgrace. These tales, as well as that of Lucie's
reader, the dying young mother, have much of the Victorian
melodrama with its sentimental morality and cathartic sense
of pathos. Yet there is also a nascent feminism, a protest
against the "physiological fatality" that dogs women's lives

and punishes them so severely for sins that are merely peccadilloes when committed by men.

Lucie Delarue-Mardrus had a somewhat conflicted relationship with the organized feminism of her day. The feminist paper *La Fronde* was launched in 1897, and daringly announced itself on the front page as "a daily newspaper of literature and politics directed, edited, managed, written and composed by women." Started by Marguerite Durand, formerly of the Comédie Française, and editor of *Figaro*'s literary supplement, it was clearly Dreyfusard in its politics. With a mixture of naiveté and audacity, and knowing nothing whatever about the radical and feminist stance of the paper, Lucie brought Marguerite Durand an account of a reading of Hélène Vacaresco's poetry. It was accepted for publication and its author was astonished and embarrassed to receive thirty francs for her article, the first money she had ever earned. It struck her as somewhat dishonorable that a work of the intellect should be recompensed in gold coin. Invited to attend the *Fronde*'s first soirée, her main concern was what to wear—she settled on a pale blue satin number belonging to one of her sister's, decorated with lace and a plunging neckline—being ignorant of the type of people who would be invited to such an event. She knew that the Dreyfus Affair was raging in Paris, splitting families and dividing salons, and that the men of her own family thundered against "the traitor, Dreyfus," but it was not until she heard the name of Joseph Reinach announced (Dreyfus's principle defender) that she realized she was in a Dreyfusard stronghold. "Papa must never know!" she said to herself (Delarue-Mardrus 1938: 97) and resolved never to return to the *Fronde*.

"I am antifeminist," she declared at that time, and her

innocence, or naiveté, were taken advantage of by editors and journalists of the day who wanted to refute the feminist cause. Thus Henri de Jouvenel (later to become Colette's second husband), editor of *Le Matin,* invited her to write a frivolous antifeminist article entitled "Du Chignon au červeau" (From the topknot to the brain), for which she received many angry letters from women readers (Delarue-Mardrus 1938: 154). Liane de Pougy describes Delarue-Mardrus as "adorable, childlike . . . little suited to the practicalities of life" (1977: 280), the very portrait of feminine dependency. Yet, de Pougy adds approvingly "she was able—fortunately—to free herself from her husband and since that experience has never attempted a second marriage or the conquest of another man" (280). It seems that as she lost the protection of her father's house and her husband's status, and was forced to leave her nebulous, poetic cloud and notice what went on around her, Delarue-Mardrus became more feminist and acquired a healthy understanding of the value of working for one's living.

"Oh this war! Basically, it is the male who dreams it up and carries it out. If there were only women on earth none of this would happen," (Harry 1946: 159), she stormed with uncharacteristic bitterness in a letter to her friend Myriam Harry during the Second World War. Or rather, it was a comment uncharacteristic of the young, wide-eyed Lucie, who placed her father's opinions before her own and boasted of knowing nothing about politics. In a moment of despair at the agonies of war, she raged,

I return to my favorite idea: castrating all men at birth. Keeping only a few in each region, carefully trained with the sole function of reproduction. The castrati would be sufficient to ensure the work necessary to human life and the women would deal with everything else. (Harry 1946: 159–160)

Strong stuff for a declared antifeminist, but like many women of her class and era, Delarue-Mardrus grew more political with age, as youth and beauty no longer brought her the advantages she had previously enjoyed without thinking.

The Angel and the Perverts, although not specifically feminist, nevertheless poses a number of questions regarding gender identity and gender roles. As a man, Marion can go where he likes, when he likes. He is free to take public transport if he wishes, stroll along the banks of the Seine at night without fear or escort. As a woman, on the other hand, she is constantly pursued by male suitors and is restricted to the private realm of taxis and domestic interiors (despite the blurring of gender divisions in the lesbian and gay milieux). Yet we are told that the transformation from female to male requires but a few gestures and may be accomplished in less than five minutes. This distinction between the outward appearance, so easily donned and doffed, and the more limited social possibilities for each sex is most clearly captured in Marion's decision to fix her gender identity by becoming a mother rather than a monk. In either case the institution, motherhood or the Catholic church, desexualizes the adherent and provides a cloak of uniformity so that the individual is reduced in importance, and institutional membership is made more prominent. It would have been relatively easy for Marion to choose either of the two paths, yet once the decision is made, her whole life will be determined by the role she must now play. In the penultimate scene, before she takes the child and becomes a mother, we see her cutting chunks off her former life, giving up her bachelor flat, deciding never again to visit her theatrical friends. She is taking the necessary steps toward entering the institution, for it is the institution, not her anatomy, that will create her gender.

ANNA LIVIA

Notes

1. In the back of this book readers will find a comprehensive bibliography of Delarue-Mardrus's works, including novels, poetry, travel books, biographies, and translations. Although it is comprehensive, I cannot claim that the list is exhaustive. In her seventy-one-year lifespan, Delarue-Mardrus wrote over seventy books and some may well have fallen prey to the erratic record keeping of a pre-computer age. The first, a collection of poetry entitled *Occident,* was published in 1901 when she was twenty-seven; the last, *Nos Secrèes amours,* the love poems she wrote for Natalie Clifford Barney in 1903, Barney had published anonymously in 1957, twelve years after the author's death. I have compiled this bibliography of Delarue-Mardrus' work from those produced by Hélène Plat in her *Lucie Delarue-Mardrus: Une Femme de lettres des années folles,* by Pauline Newman-Gordon in her entry on Lucie Delarue-Mardrus in the "bio-bibliographical sourcebook," *French Women Writers;* from the data provided by the Firstsearch bibliographical database; and from information given in Lucie Delarue-Mardrus's own memoirs. For the publishers I have given the names of the presses which issued Delarue-Mardrus's works in book form; readers should bear in mind, however, that the vast majority of her fiction was first published in serial form in the journals and magazines of the day. (Though this does not appear to have been the case with *The Angel and the Perverts.*)

   To anyone contemplating further research on Lucie Delarue-Mardrus I would commend Plat's biography (alas not yet translated) for the painstaking work she has done in tracking down Lucie's friends, distant relatives, former neighbors, and even children of neighbors, to produce a lively, entertaining account which concentrates particularly on Lucie's social life and celebrity acquaintances. Newman-Gordon's thirteen-page account, on the other hand, focuses

on Lucie's literary works in a more academic presentation. Newman-
Gordon has explored the major themes of Delarue-Mardrus's fiction
and provides an admirable section on the contemporary reception of
her work. For the scholar more interested in "eye-witness" accounts,
Delarue-Mardrus's own memoirs will be essential reading though,
again, the book has not been translated. She provides a wealth of
information on the genesis and publication of her various novels and
poetry collections, as well as anecdotes and vignettes of the people
she knew. Myriam Harry's *Mon amie, Lucie Delarue-Mardrus* describes in warm, personal detail her friendship with the author, adding a valuable picture of the time Delarue-Mardrus spent in North
Africa, since Harry and her husband knew the same people and
traveled in the same circles. Barney's portrait concentrates on Lucie
and Joseph-Charles Mardrus as a couple. The book from which this
account comes is entitled *Souvenirs indiscrets* (Indiscreet memories)
and it is therefore not surprising, perhaps, that Barney is particularly
interested in telling the world about the more salacious aspects of her
relationship with Monsieur and Madame Mardrus. She tends to wan-
der from the point in a rather disconcerting way, however, and often
recounts anecdotes from her own life, which appear to have no connection to that of either Lucie or Joseph-Charles. She also has the
bad habit of quoting whole pages at a time from Lucie's memoirs,
occasioning much repetition between the two accounts.

2. Here is the poem in its entirety.

L'odeur de mon pays était dans une pomme.
Je l'ai mordue, avec les yeux fermés du somme,
Pour me croire debout dans un herbage vert,
L'herbe haute sentait le soleil et la mer.
L'ombre des peupliers y allongeait des raies
Et j'entendais le bruit des oiseaux, plein les haies,
Se mêler au retour des vagues de midi.
Je venais de hocher le pommier arrondi
Et je m'inquiétais d'avoir laissé ouverte
Derrière moi la porte au toit de chaume mou . . .
Combien de fois aussi l'automne rousse et verte
Me vit-elle, au milieu du soleil, et debout,
Manger, les yeux fermés la pomme rebondie
De tes prés, copieuse et forte Normandie? . . .
Ah! je ne me guérirai jamais de mon pays!
N'est-il pas la douceur des feuillages cueillis

Dans leur fraîcheur, la paix et toute l'innoncence?
Et qui donc a jamais guéri de son enfance? (from *Ferveur*)

3. It was the custom of the day to refer to servants by their first names only. I regret that I do not know Berthe's last name. Readers should, however, not confuse her with Berthe Cleyrergue, who was Natalie Barney's housekeeper for more than fifty years.

4. "After the death of the author." The idea has become such a hypnotic linchpin of contemporary criticism that it seems to beg for latinate recognition.

5. Even the blessed simplicity of counting may not insure homogeneous results. There are seven titled volumes in Proust's *A la recherche du temps perdu*, but, because each is very long, publishers often further subdivide them. Thus a full set often reaches as many as fifteen separate books.

6. I owe this analogy to Veronica O'Donovan with whom I had an animated discussion about the high and popular cultures of Paris in the Belle Epoque and the *années folles*.

7. *Infra dig.*, abbreviation for *infra dignitatem* or "beneath one's dignity."

8. Take as read a reference to Michel Foucault's *La Volonté de savoir* and the importance of both confession and medical examination to the bourgeois order.

9. According to recent figures, the incidence of some degree of hermaphroditism may be as high as 4 percent of all newborns (Epstein 1990: 100 and note 6). In assigning gender to an intersexed infant doctors pay more attention to the size of the penis than to any other criterion, hormonal or anatomical. Suzanne Kessler quotes, for example, from interviews she conducted with six medical experts in intersexuality, "The formulation 'good penis equals male; absence of good penis equals female' is treated in the literature and by the physicians interviewed as an objective criterion, operative in all cases" Kessler 1990: 20. Elsewhere she observes, "Money states the fundamental rule for gender assignment: 'Never assign a baby to be reared . . . as a boy unless the phallic structure . . . is neonatally of at least the same caliber as that of same-aged males with small-average penises' " (ibid: 18). In the euphemistic language of *The Angel and the Perverts*, Marion's lack of a beard symbolizes the lack of an adequate penis.

It is interesting to note that in the *"Que sais-je"* volume on transsexuals, Talmudic law is quoted as prohibiting marriage between a hermaphrodite, or an "either-man-or-woman" *(ou-bien-homme-ou-bien-femme)*, and a man. If the hermaphrodite were a man, the partners would be transgressing the Biblical ban on homosexuality. If the hermaphrodite were a woman, on the other hand, her marriage to another woman would simply be void (Pettiti 1992: 118). (That there should already be a volume on transsexuality in the *"Que sais-je"* series, an encyclopedic collection of booklets on such issues as the Channel tunnel, French slang, North African literature, used mostly by French students to cram for exams, is interesting in itself.) Whether the hermaphrodites' anatomy or their sexual orientation is taken into consideration, it is always the masculine element which is decisive.

10. Take as read a reference to the work of Judith Butler on gender as a performative: *Gender Trouble* (Routledge 1990) or *Bodies That Matter* (Routledge 1993), whichever.

References

Where two dates appear, the first is the date of first publication, the second the edition that I have used in this study and to which page numbers therefore refer.

Barnes, Djuna (1928, 1993). *Ladies Almanack*. New York: New York University Press.

Barney, Natalie Clifford (1902). *Cinq Petits Dialogues grecs*. Paris: Plume.

———(1910). *Eparpillements*. Paris: Sansot.

———(1920). *Pensées d'une amazone*. Paris: Emile-Paul.

———(1930) *The One Who Is Legion, or A.D.'s Afterlife*. London: Partridge.

———(1960). *Souvenirs indiscrets*. Paris: Flammarion.

Benjamin, Walter (1968). *Illuminations: Essays and Reflections*. New York: Schocken Books.

Billy, André (1951). *L'Epoque 1900*. Paris: Tallandier.

Butler, Judith (1990). *Gender Trouble*. London: Routledge.

———(1993). *Bodies That Matter*. London: Routledge.

Chalon, Jean (1976, 1992). *Chère Natalie Barney*. Paris: Flammarion.

Colette (1903, 1972). *Claudine s'en va*. Paris: Livre de Poche.

———(1931, 1971) *Le Pur et l'impur*. Paris: Livre de Poche.

Delarue-Mardrus (1908). *Marie, fille-mère*. Paris: Fasquelle.

———(1909). *Le Roman de six petites filles*. Paris: Fasquelle.

———(1919). *L'Ame aux trois visages*. Paris: Gédalge.

———(1925). *Hortensia dégénérée*. Paris: Fasquelle.

———(1929). *Les Amours d'Oscar Wilde*. Paris: Flammarion.

———(1935). *Une Femme mûre et l'amour*. Paris: Fasquelle.

———(1938). *Mes mémoires*. Paris: Gallimard.

———(1957). *Nos secrètes amours*. Paris: Les Isles.

Epstein, Julia (1990). "Either/Or—Neither/Both: Sexual Ambiguity and the Ideology of Gender." In *Genders,* No. 7.

Foucault, Michel (1976). *La Volonté de savoir*. Paris: Gallimard.

———(1978). *Herculine Barbin dite Alexina B.* Paris: Gallimard.

Hall, Radclyffe (1928, 1990). *The Well of Loneliness*. New York: Bantam, Doubleday, Dell.

Harry, Myriam (1946). *Mon amie, Lucie Delarue-Mardrus*. Paris: Ariane.

Jay, Karla (1988). *The Amazon and the Page*. Bloomington: Indiana University Press.

Kessler, Suzanne (1990). "The Medical Construction of Gender: Case Management of Intersexed Infants." In *Signs,* vol. 16, no. 1.

Newman-Gordon, Pauline (1991). "Lucie Delarue-Mardrus." In Sartori, Eva Martin, and Dorothy Wynne Zimmerman (eds.). *French Women Writers: A Bio-Bibliographical Source Book*. New York: Greenwood Press.

Pettiti, Louis-Edmond (1992). *Les Transsexuels*. Paris: Presses universitaires de France, "Que sais-je?" series.

Plat, Hélène (1994). *Lucie Delarue-Mardrus: Une Femme de lettres des années folles*. Paris: Grasset.

Pougy, Liane de (1901, 1979). *Idylle sapphique*. Paris: J C Lattès.

———(1977). *Mes cahiers bleus*. Paris: Plon.

Réval, Gabrielle (1924). *La Chaîne des dames*. Paris: Crès.

Stein, Gertrude (1950). *Things As They Are*. Banyan Press.

Vivien, Renée (1904a, 1983). *La Dame à la louve*. New York: Gay Presses of New York.

———(1904a, 1977). *Une Femme m'apparut*. Paris: Desforges.

Woolf, Virginia (1928, 1956). *Orlando*. New York: Harcourt, Brace, Jovanovich.

The Angel and the Perverts

[I]

He often dreamed that his mother, or rather the blind beast which works within us independently of our minds, had been expecting twins while she was carrying him, for, ever since the age when human beings enter into the agony of the soul, he had felt instinctively at his side a mysterious second self.

The fine lady with the reticent eyes, who carried the distinction and stiffness of her race in her very marrow, insisted from the cradle onward that she alone would look after the sickly creature she had brought into the world. She never left the child in the hands of an underling, even for a minute. A rare quality for an Anglo-Saxon woman, especially one of high class. Later she continued to wash, dress, play with him, and put him to bed without any help from a nanny. It was from her he learned his first prayers, and to read, write, and count in English and French.

In France at least this would suppose the most intense tenderness between mother and son. But the dry kiss with which the tot was greeted each morning and sent away each evening was enough to maintain a terrible distance between them. The formality of playtime was chilling:

"Play!" Madame de Valdeclare would order.

And if occasionally, on rainy days, she would condescend to play a few games of snakes and ladders, no familiarity accompanied this pastime.

It seems very probable that the father, a hard, taciturn man, imposed such a child-rearing system on his wife, terrorizing her into the bargain. It was clear that he fled the sight of his only offspring, in whom he inspired a monstrous terror. A hostile stranger would not have looked at the poor child with greater malevolence.

Occasionally the boy would be taken for a drive in the car Hervin de Valdeclare used to visit his farms, or to journey as far as Paris where he had business with various lawyers. As they passed through endless plains of beetroot, which none of them bothered to look at, the child would cling to his mother and keep his head stubbornly lowered to avoid glimpsing the face of the gentleman with the long moustache whose son he was.

The first *abbé* to come to the *château,* an arrogant old ecclesiastic brought back from Paris after a short business trip, did nothing to alleviate the régime to which one of the gentlest little boys on earth had been subjected.

So be it. All parents are distant and suspicious, all priests toothless and surly, all children treated like guilty prisoners.

Both delicate and hardy, the little boy alternated between

his bed and the schoolroom, would catch up a month's illness in three days. At times they would have to restrain the feverish eagerness with which he learned his lessons and did his homework, while at others he had to be punished for his laziness.

Kept implacably away from other children, he did not even go to catechism lessons when the time came, but received that pious instruction from the *abbé*. He was forbidden to speak to the servants. He could not play without supervision. The *abbé's* reign did nothing to end this jealous surveillance. The slender Englishwoman sat silently through every lesson, accompanied them on every walk. And at night the little lad slept in a small room next to hers.

Deprived of any intimacy with the repressed individuals who peopled his world, brought up on hard work, coldness, and enigma, he turned his gaze toward the void, full of the questions and absurdity of childhood. His great eyes, in which three distinct colors could be seen laid out like a rose window, were shadowed by the prominent ridges of his eyebrows, which stood out upon a forehead rich in intellect.

With his thin fingers and a face consumed by pallor, his whole slender being bore that air of pathos which marks the beauty of the invalid.

"Mother," [1] he would say. *Mamma* would have been too gentle for this child whom no one loved. No one called him "tu." He had no dog. No cat. His only friend was the unborn double who obsessed and defied him all at once, demonic familiar of this troubled, troubling being.

Since he was never alone, it was only when preparing his lessons for the *abbé*, or when he was in bed that he could call up the phantom's presence.

We forget so many of the dreams of our early years and

no one is there to record them in time. The visionary creations of childhood, and of some childhoods more than others, would prove to be masterpieces of poetry or fantasy for one who could write them down in a language close enough to their conception.

The little Valdeclare lowered his eyes hypocritically over the page and, speechless, chattered with his mute other, his invisible brother. The games of his imagination whirled around inside his head, veritable creations in which the genius of those tender years overflowed. The delights, quarrels, and poetic enthusiasms of his imagination caused such a range of expressions to pass over his absorbed countenance that his mother would ask in alarm, "What is the matter, Marion?"[2]

She pronounced it "Marion," an English name which can be used for either sex. The little boy would jump, woken with a start as though from sleep. No plausible explanation came to mind. He had been bent over an arithmetic problem! He would look fearfully at the woman sewing on the other side of the table who was secretly watching him. Quickly he would improvise: "I was thinking about *Monsieur l'abbé*. He nearly fell over yesterday when he was throwing me the ball. Didn't you see?"

But he hated that ball, officially sanctioned recreation with no room for the fantastic or the intangible. He had been given it the previous Christmas instead of the doll he had asked for. Nor was he allowed to cut out figures in gold and colored paper. He got no pleasure from a wooden puzzle or a little mechanical car. The only toy he enjoyed was an old kaleidoscope which had been in the family for years. He was amazed to the point of terror that they let him vanish into that little fairyland. "If I look into it too often, they'll take it away from me." He did not realize what a martyrdom his childhood was. He would have liked to hide away so he could play with the marvelous toy, feeling as though he were doing something forbidden. But there was nowhere to hide.

His favorite ritual of the day was going to bed. It was true his mother could see him from her bedside, her eyes burning in the shadow of the nightlight. But, turning toward the wall, he experienced a moment of inexpressible release. He was two once again, and he smiled at his brother. Unfortunately he would doze off too fast. But before slipping into that end of everything which we call sleep, he had time to confide his secrets. One baby word remained in his private vocabulary. He would list the day's sorrows:

"Bobo,[3] the story of the unlearned lesson . . . Bobo, the story of playing ball when I didn't want to . . . Bobo, the story of Father on the stairs . . . "

And, on certain evenings, this cry of utter despair, "Bobo, the story of everything!"

As he grew up, he stopped dreaming so much and threw himself into his studies. At fourteen he wrote Latin poetry as though it were child's play, knew several plays by Racine and Corneille by heart, was beginning integral calculus, polishing up his knowledge of botany, had started astronomy, spoke fluent English, and was reading the German poets. They had had to find a new *abbé*. One after another his successors gave up on this all-consuming pupil.

"He'll become a Benedictine!" they would say in alarm.

The first time this word was spoken, Marion witnessed a miracle: a smile on Madame de Valdeclare's tight lips.

A little later she asked him what his intentions were. If he wanted to go to the seminary, they would not stand in his way.

At table his father went so far as to address him directly.

"The best thing you could do would be to become a priest!"

He made no reply. He so seldom spoke! Then a veritable siege began around that adolescent boy. The *abbé,* the village priest for whom he'd been serving mass for the last six years, his mother, even his father all clamored:

"Seminary! Seminary!"

But the daily surveillance grew worse, not better.

He endured it as he had when he was little, but now he felt himself to be superior to that old Protestant woman, the shrunken figure whose hair was already grey, who went on sewing soundlessly amid his books, gentle tyrant with an English accent. Whenever he lifted his eyes to her face, she would turn hers away. Sometimes he would throw back his seraphic head and watch her without speaking. A moment's silent insolence. Embarrassed, she would cough and in a voice which became more and more hesitant, would ask, "What is the matter, Marion?"[4]

But he no longer even deigned to reply.

Fifteen years old. His sinister childhood was over. He was about to enter the age of independence. He was impatient for the day when cowardice would yield to manly vigor. What shame it was to feel so timorous!

He tried obsessively to catch glimpses of himself in the mirror, would feel his hairless upper lip furtively. The first hairs of his moustache would be a signal for revolution throughout his being. His heart beat fast at the idea.

"We'll let them see what men we are!" he boasted nightly to his shadow twin.

For his father he felt a most particular hatred, that maleficent idler forever locked away in his useless office.

"The seminary will be our escape route from this house. Then he'll see! And the *abbé?* . . . And Mother?[5] What will they all say?"

He laughed into his pillow, the solitary laugh to which he had been condemned, a sickly mirth that he stifled as though it were indecent. And suddenly the laugh would stop, a sigh too big for him would fill his throat.

"Bobo, the story of the moustache which will not grow!"

Then, suddenly, death.

The first day that she took to her bed, Mother[6] called for her son.

This had happened before. He would then have to work at her bedside for as long as she was laid up. The *abbé,* who could not enter the room, would wait until she was better before resuming his lessons.

But the *abbé* did not wait. He packed his bags and fled one morning as soon as it was announced that she had influenza. He had heard this was infectious, which it was indeed.

Seeing two diamonds in the dying woman's eyes, Marion bent over the bed. Mother[7] took hold of his hands and grasped them in hers, moved by an extraordinary force. He heard her utter, "My poor poor child!"[8]

Remorse at last! Tenderness *in extremis!*

For the first time in his life he cried out, "Mamma!"

But she was no longer alive to hear it. Lost in death and incomprehension he turned toward his father standing motionless at the foot of the bed and caught his look of hatred. The man's lips moved, "You have made her suffer enough, the poor woman."

"Me?" he exclaimed with a sob.

Two figures in black in the over-large dining room: father and son having a *tête-à-tête.*

"I cannot look after you. Your mother needed to be here for that."

"Yes," said Marion, in tones like a boy's voice breaking.

"It's impossible for me to stay here alone. I have to go away, travel abroad. But all the same, I can't very well send you to the Jesuits!"

"Why, Father? . . . Why, Father?"

Intense hope had just called out to him. Other schoolboys! Oh to get away from the *château,* from the beet fields! To live!

"Because."

The grim mouth snapped shut. Silence.

One day he would understand the despair with which his mother had doubtless loved him, an anxious dog guarding her little one against wild beasts—and such beasts!

As he was leaving college—leaving hell—(bearing every possible diploma and without having seen his father again, even during vacation, since the latter had abruptly decided on the Jesuits) he learned that he was an orphan, heir to the northern *château* which had been bombed during the war, and to what little remained of his family's wealth.

He had always been alone in the world. He set off bitterly upon the road to life, accompanied by his double, his strange, ill-starred double—the taint of his birth.

[II]

"It's no use bothering her. She cares for nothing and no one."

The voice of Laurette Wells remained cool and self-possessed as she pronounced these words, a most ironic expression of anger. She rewrapped her legs in the ermine blanket, pulling it out from under Janine who was curled up at the foot of the bed. Her steely eyes sent out sparks in the moonlight of her bedroom, which looked brighter than ever that evening.

The play of the mirrors, the Venetian chandelier, the great quantities of rare crystal, decked the silhouettes of the furniture and the white animal skins with icicles of reflected light.

A trace of perfume floated in the bluish meanders of the air, drifting up from the third member of the group who was smoking continually. The bare windows, looking out on the garden at five o'clock in the afternoon, were black with winter.

The contralto voice of the woman sitting motionless, smoking a little way off from the others, gave Laurette and Janine a start. It was hard to get used to those deep tones, which broke with bizarre suddenness.

"Did you hear that, Janine? I care for nothing and no one. Perfectly put."

"Oh really!" Janine protested. "You're not trying to make us believe . . ."

The girl with the hoarse voice was resigned.

"Of course. I knew you wouldn't give up!"

Before settling back in the violet armchair, she stretched her large hand toward the cigarettes laid out on the Chinese table. That momentary glimpse of her profile displayed the cut of her hair, like a gleaming helmet, well-chiseled features, and a thin, extremely sorrowful mouth. It also showed up her lightly powdered eye lid, her prominent brow, in whose shadow dwelled the three different blues of her eyes.

Janine began to pout.

"You care for nothing and no one! What a pity! A beautiful young lady like you!"

"Who said I was a young lady?"

The graceful young thing lying sprawled out at the foot of the bed now gazed in fascination at those eyes of triple blue. Then Marion laughed. She put her fist to her mouth to stifle the sound which had no right to come out: a horrible childhood memory, a thing half-born that makes people shudder.

Once it was over, she said, "Guess what I am?"

"An archangel!" Janine cried earnestly. "A beautiful archangel who has come down to earth to visit us!"

"And who will fly off again in a hurry," Laurette scolded
under her breath, "if you keep on asking him to tea in that
ridiculous fashion. Archangels do not go to tea with little
divorcées. Leave her alone, all of you. I've told you, she cares
for nothing and no one."

"She does not care for you . . . It's not the same thing."

"Nor for you."

Marion, her tailored suit tight against her narrow hips,
legs crossed, was smoking, her thoughts elsewhere.

"Janine, are you going home on foot tonight?"

"Yes. It's just next door. Do you want to come with me?"

"Oh no! . . . Absolutely not!" Marion cried, her English
accent still evident, while Laurette, brought up in our boarding schools, spoke French without any trace of a British
accent.

"Why do you ask if I'm going home alone, Marion?"

"Because I noticed something in Laurette's garden which
you too will see as you pass the arc lamp in the moonlight.
Stand still a moment next to the bush, you know, the one by
the bend in the main avenue? Even here in Neuilly. . . .[1] Soon
you'll see someone's shadow coming toward you along the
ground. You'll look up to see who it is, but you won't see
anyone, because there won't be anyone there. The shadow
will walk along the ground all by itself."

"Oh I like that!" said Laurette, who was a poet.

But Janine shivered, "I'm scared! I'll never dare walk
across the park now! Come with me, Marion!"

"You would be much more frightened with her. I'll let you
have the driver."

Janine got up sadly and put on her coat.

"It's rotten that I have to go home to have tea at my house . . . And it's rotten that Marion won't come with me!"

"Pretty, don't you think? . . ." said Laurette after she had gone.

"Very."

"Why so cold to her, Marion?"

"Why should I be otherwise? She doesn't interest me."

"Me neither! So superficial . . . And, purely from the physical point of view, she leaves something to be desired."

"Not even that!" Marion exclaimed, lighting up another cigarette. "Someone who left something to be desired, how wonderful! That way one could make up the rest. How good it must feel to desire someone!"

"You're thirty years old, Marion, and you've never wanted anyone?"

"No."

"You left that task to others when they were looking at you."

"Unfortunately, yes!"

"Don't get your hunted look. I'm not the others. These last four years I've known when to stop."

"You haven't learned all that well; otherwise you'd stop asking me these questions."

Tea was brought in. They switched to English in front of the servant. Alone once more, they went back to French.

"Why?" Marion remarked. "You're American and I'm half English."

"That's just it. The truth is easier in a foreign language. It's like wearing a mask."

"You're as fond of the truth as that?"

"It depends on who I'm with."

"And you've chosen me?"

Laurette's left eyebrow rose slowly, a sign of surprise or emotion to those who knew her well. Pink and white, her hair dressed with spun glass, her cold energy could only be seen in her thick eyebrows, in the sturdy ridge of her fleshy, slightly hooked nose, in the outline of her sensual mouth with their beautiful white teeth, and lips which twitched up at the corners when she smiled, giving a sudden mocking cast to her face.

She had the rounded lines of a very feminine body, hair like a fairy's, a soft voice, and she blushed self-consciously. As though with careful craft, a delicious crayon blended the surprise in her eyes into a sword blade, which sparkled with intelligence, sarcasm, and strong will. Those eyes seemed to see only one thing at a time, but they took in everything.

Marion put down her cup, opened her purse and retouched her lipstick before lighting another cigarette. Absently, Laurette pushed the candies toward her; she had been picking them up and eating them without choosing amongst them, as though they were morsels of bread. The box was soon empty. Still lying on the bed, her face in Marion's ear-length hair, Laurette murmured: "Thank you, Marion, for being what you are. I thought I was no longer capable of suffering, and you have given me back that ability."

"Don't be so melodramatic," said Marion. "Such noble suffering is easily consoled. The room would be full if one included only your latest victims, not counting Janine, who, you say, does not interest you."

"Janine . . . Oh yes . . . I love the shape of her nostrils!"

"I know! I know! You are the Greek sculptor who makes one statue out of the features of twenty different women. Janine's nostrils have served you just like the eyes of the woman in the train. You probably don't even remember what you told me, two years ago, when you got back from Constantinople."

"No, Marion."

"I was asking you about your impressions of the trip . . . Why did you go to Constantinople in the first place?"

"Yes . . . Why did I go to Constantinople?"

"Doubtless no one will ever know, not even yourself. You see nothing when you travel but the details of the faces around you. In any case, you said to me, 'Turkey? . . . A young girl got into my compartment and she made me forget why I had left. I loved how her eyes were set in her head!' "

Laurette began to laugh her famous laugh, almost as soft as her voice, but whose sudden gaiety was as honest as a child's.

"Oh Marion! How I love you!"

Marion considered her for a moment with a curious look in her eye.

"You love me because you know very well I will not put up with your pretentious sentimentality. You find it re-laxing."

In the face of attack or criticism, Laurette's response was always elegant.

"My sentiments are frivolous, I know. But one can only give what is asked of one. With you I am quite simple, Marion."

"Perhaps. When there's no one else around."

"Why do you do people the honor of your presence on occasion?"

"Oh, here it comes! Because I like eggs with clear yolks."

"Eggs with clear yolks! How pretty! What does it mean?"

"It means infertile eggs which will never produce anything."

"Really? . . . And why does that appeal to you?"

"Because one always likes that which one resembles."

"But Marion, you don't have a clear yolk! Someone who can write the two plays you read to me . . ."

"Which will never be performed . . ."

"What does that matter? It doesn't stop them existing."

"Laurette, I hope you will never speak of them again to anyone! I read them to you on that condition. But you went and told everyone . . ."

"You know very well I am like a secret lock. The mechanism is so complicated it is easier to open than the others."

"Yes, I realize that now. That's why I'll never tell you another thing."

"Marion! It is a shame to keep such beautiful writing for me alone. There is genius in your plays. When will you read them here? I'll invite theater people, artists, critics . . ."

"Laurette, you're impossible! Why do I have to keep telling you that I do not want people to know I write plays?"

"Darling, people *must* know."

Marion, so pale already, grew paler still. She knew that the soft voice could go on indefinitely repeating things it had been forbidden to say. Marion hit the arm of the violet armchair with her fist. Her anger was contagious and Laurette's eyes, which had suddenly gone hard, grew darker.

"When one is what you are, one should not keep silent. Superiority must have its place as well as stupidity. You . . ."

"I'm leaving!" said Marion, getting to her feet. "I know you'll go on harping about it until tomorrow morning. Your stupendous obstinacy may be the sincerest of your vices, which latter I only half believe in despite all you do to make them known."

"No!" Laurette begged. "Don't go! You're not going to leave me all alone with my vices?"

"It's not such bad company . . ."

"What if I prefer yours?"

"It's amusing when you play the ladies' man," Marion said in her hoarse voice. "Especially with me. It's funny."

"Why?"

"Because . . ."

A silence fell, during which each of them doubtless went over all the things one never says, even when involved in a heart-to-heart. Laurette was the first to speak again, her eyes soft, her cheeks blushing.

"Do I have as many vices as that, Marion?"

"A few, Laurette," Marion replied, sitting down again. "Or perhaps only one, but you definitely have all the character flaws."

Laurette looked at her, subdued. No one ever heard her defend herself, even when wrongly accused, a rare thing.

Abruptly, in a low voice, as though her sense of decency fought against it, Marion declared, "But you are the only person in the world I care for even a little."

"Darling . . ." Laurette murmured.

"You are perverse," Marion went on with muted indignation, "dissolute, self-centered, unfair, stubborn, sometimes miserly, often play-acting, irritating most of the time . . . a monster, in fact. But you are a genuine rebel, ever ready to incite others to rebellion. At heart, a good sort. Perhaps I am wrong but I am sure that if I, or another of your friends, were arrested one day, let's say for theft, you would be there, and it would not affect your friendship in the least because you are capable of loving someone just as they are, even a thief—in this lies your only fidelity. And so you have my respect."

Laurette was listening attentively, summing her up in a low voice as though to herself: "You are certainly the most mysterious woman I know, Marion . . ."

"Perhaps . . ."

"You are young and beautiful and you want nothing to do with love. You have enormous talent and you don't want anyone to know about it. As for your life, no one has any idea what it's like. I have known you for four years and I know nothing about you—nothing but the essentials," she added with her prettiest smile.

"The essentials . . ." Marion mused.

"Yes . . . I know you love music, beauty, the arts, independence, that you have read everything, studied everything, that you know everything, that you can do so many things . . . I know that you're bitter, sad . . ."

"No. I have invented my own happiness without other people. That's all."

"Happiness which has given you that desolate look about the mouth . . ."

Marion got to her feet in one bound.

"That's another story!"

The little felt hat was pulled down over the glossy hair,

the suit disappeared under the broadcloth of her coat, cut like a man's overcoat.

"Laurette, I heard you say earlier that you were dining out and that you were expected at a very early hour. I must interest you considerably seeing that you have not started gazing at the doors, longing to sidle through them. For, despite your affectation of coming from nowhere, you are terribly American. Twenty-five different appointments in all corners of Paris at the same time, without counting five minutes at the theater, a quarter of an hour at a concert: a pathological case of the fidgets from all the ferries, trains, and hotels you trundled around in at too young an age, like all the little Yankees who are too rich for their own good."

Laurette let out a peal of honest laughter which seemed to put her in a state of innocence. When she had finished laughing at her own expense, she turned persuasively, caressingly to Marion: "Marion, if you'd stay here with me, I wouldn't go out to dinner, I wouldn't even know I was expected."

"No!"

At this unanswerable "No," Laurette got slowly to her feet, swathed in the white folds of her gown. She put out her hand for the cold handshake of her people. Her eyes were already looking at the clock which hung above her bed. Since Marion would not stay, she suddenly felt terribly late; for whoever she may be, an American never forgets the time.

The tall girl with the hoarse voice had already stridden away without a backward glance.

[III]

The tall girl with the hoarse voice whistled for a taxi lost in the wastes of Neuilly bordering the Seine. In the time it would take to get to the address she had given the driver, she would be able to smoke at least two cigarettes.

She settled down in the corner of the seat, lit up, and fell into thought with the bumping of the car.

The pleasure of returning to her shabby bachelor flat awaited her in a little street like a twisting medieval dragon of the Left Bank.

"My life . . ." Marion mused.

Even when there was no one to hear, her derisive laugh was quickly smothered.

Just before she arrived, she took out the little tube of Vaseline, which she used to remove her make-up. Once this task was accomplished, she closed the bag and stuffed it into the pocket of her overcoat. After she paid the driver, she had three stories to climb. The house went no higher. She glanced in at the concierge's lodge as she passed the mezzanine. At last she fit the key into her lock and she was home.

He was home.

It took but a few brief movements, contemporary feminine fashion lending itself to this kind of transformation. The time to replace her short skirt with a pair of long pants and Marion, the girl of thirty, became again the eternal youth she really was.

She let out a deep sigh of relief. When one has been brought up as a boy, it's hard, even after several years' practice, to feel at home dressed as a woman.

A quick stroke of the comb through the sleeked-down helmet of his hair and his curls were free. Looking at himself in the mirror, he saw once again the inspired seraphim of old.

Young Valdeclare was almost as unusual as an adolescent boy as Miss Hervin was as a young lady. In the end his childhood twin had turned out to be an older sister. What a real stroke of luck to have a name which could serve a dual purpose.

"I have time to eat something, and even get some work done . . ." Marion thought to himself as he sat down to the meager plate of cold meat laid out on the table.

This strange figure ate without appetite, turning over the pages of an old book with gold leaves. Books were the only luxury in his miserable dwelling, and a great luxury they were. A hard sofabed in one corner, a large wooden work table painted white, with room to eat at one end, two cane chairs, a leather armchair, a Louis XVI bureau, and the narrow room was full. The gas radiator seemed to take up an enormous amount of space. But there was no telling what the wallpaper looked like, since the walls were lined from floor to ceiling with beautifully bound tomes, reminiscent of Franciscan libraries. Next door there was a boxroom, a tiny kitchen, and that was it.

Even Miss Hervin's modest apartment in the 16th had a little more elegance.

Marion read and forgot his dinner. He also forgot that it was cold and the gas wasn't lit. The solitary electric bulb gave off a dim light. The documents he needed for his book were pretty much finished; they sat in a file on the table surrounded by piles of other papers. Pencil in hand, he underlined the passages which would be of use. The book he was working on was in verse and took place under the Directoire.[1] Young Valdeclare did the work behind well-known names from old families, eking a bitter living from this unjust labor. His opus was already considerable. He had prepared public lectures for a famous lawyer (for he had a law degree); collaborated on plays which were great hits — and for which he had done more than half the work; provided the research for two volumes of history; written the memoirs of a rich aristocrat. The small fortune left by his father was not enough to live on. As a woman he had been a shorthand/typist for a newspaper editor; as a man, he had been secretary to someone in the theater; he had written fillers for the daily papers, done some interviews. This brain-of-all-trades knew all the tricks of the literary world and found employment in every domain. Marion consoled himself for his monstrous anonymity with the independence that anonymity brings—the independence of his double life.

If anyone were to see him in both guises, he had his explanation ready: "Yes, that's my older sister," or "That's my younger brother, we look a lot alike but we had a terrible falling out. We're no longer even on speaking terms."

Unfortunately, he could not modulate his voice, which, in either persona, remained the same disconcerting yodel.

"Nine o'clock . . . ," Marion murmured, closing his book.

He got up, wrapped his scarf around his neck, put on his overcoat and felt hat, and went out.

The thin nocturnal visitor was welcomed by a wave of warmth from Julien Midalge's loft. He came in from the wintry rain to be greeted by lights, flowers, the sound of voices, a delightful evening in progress. Walking even such a short distance was bad for his delicate constitution.

"Here's Marion!" Julien Midalge exclaimed.

He performed the introductions. They exchanged small talk. All four guests had the same way of talking, words dropping languidly from pursed lips with an air of complete exhaustion. Two of them must have been wearing make-up, so brilliantly did their eyes sparkle, and all four clearly had powder on their cheeks. Only Julien, a man of forty-five, bravely sported his natural skin color: opium yellow. A big shiny nose, small black eyes, puffy eyelids, and a bald skull in no way impeded his habit of aping the mannerisms of others, or perhaps it was the others who were copying him. He was wearing green pajamas decorated with flowery Arab designs and a gold bracelet on his wrist. He looked a complete clown. Pretty soon, however, his young guests began to compliment him.

"My dear, how simply splendid!" said one as he fingered the cloth.

"You have to hand it to him!" said a second.

A third: "Who makes your pajamas for you?"

A fourth: "You know he never gives out his addresses!"

Marion alone remained silent, watched furtively by the others. The blue of his eyes, set out like the petals of a rose, his delicate pallor, the despair around his mouth, had immediately had their effect. Now the discussion grew more animated as they sat down in armchairs or stretched out on divans in the diffuse lighting, between exquisitely arranged bouquets of flowers centered around the pedestal table which held the port and biscuits. The names of shirt-makers were passed around, then the names of boot-makers and hat-makers. Exclamations followed. They insisted on all chattering at the same time like women launched on the subject of clothes. There were only two foreigners, but the three Frenchmen spoke with an accent, the accent invented by Parisian snobs to make them sound cosmopolitan.

They could not tell whether Marion, lost in smoke, was listening to this verbiage. Though it was for his benefit that they were going to such pains. When a cat fight broke out, all eyes turned to him, but he did not even smile.

"Monsieur de Valdeclare is sad . . . ," observed the one called Totote.

"No!" Midalge replied. "He is lost in reverie. Quite another matter."

"I really could not imagine the romantic poet any other way," said Emilio, the Argentinean, gyrating in his seat.

"Absolutely . . ." agreed another emphatically, himself so blond, so pink, so transparent he was the image of Scandinavia. "I was thinking the exact same thing myself."

"Except that I'm not a poet," Marion snorted. "Still less a romantic!"

His voice and his laugh generated the usual surprise.

"That's what he says . . . But I've heard him recite some quite admirable poetry," Midalge revealed. "Written anonymously, but clearly his own work. Tonight, if he were willing . . ."

"What a treat that would be!" Marion retorted coldly, "With my beautiful voice . . ."

"I've never seen anything so moving . . ." murmured the small dark-haired man, who had been devouring him silently with his eyes. "On the contrary, it must be quite sublime to hear you recite . . . Oh! That broken sob caught in your throat!"

Marion gave his categorical *no!*

"An untamed soul . . ." Totote declared admiringly.

"And so mysterious!" Midalge finished for him in an undertone. "What did I tell you?"

"Not again!" Marion exclaimed.

"What do you mean, again?"

"I beg your pardon. I've already been treated to all this earlier today."

"Where?" two voices demanded.

"Don't imagine he'll ever let you know what goes on in his life!" Midalge warned them.

All five of them gazed at him, intrigued. He let them stare, enigmatic and cold as ice, smoking his cigarette as though he were alone in the exquisite furnishings of the loft.

Midalge, quite gay at times, asked with an air of amuse-ment, "Why does he come and see me from time to time, I wonder?"

Totote grew bold. "The beautiful sphinx comes amongst us only to be admired."

And as Marion shrugged, the small dark-haired man said passionately, "I love his silence."

Gradually they all began to talk about him in his presence, as though he did not understand French.

Then, suddenly, Marion rounded on them, "I come to see you because . . . You think I'm the strange beast. Well, it's entirely the other way round!"

There were muffled protests, mingled with laughter.

"Charming boy!" muttered Emilio.

But the small dark-haired man was roused, his nostrils flaring, "Let him be what he is! Let him speak! . . . Let him speak! . . ."

"You want me to tell you?" Marion continued, consumed with rage which he forced himself not to let show. "I've already made this speech once today . . . (Oh yes, I know!) So here it is: You interest me because you are eggs with clear yolks, you know, infertile eggs. I have a penchant for them, that's all. It amuses me to watch women in Paris who behave like men and men who behave like women. To me there is no more ridiculous sight than a false hermaphrodite."

They waited, nonplussed, their mouths open. Marion was already familiar with that attentive frown which means, "Whatever is that?" He had seen it on many different faces, each time he felt like sowing unease.

"Hmmph . . . ," Midalge grunted, somewhat embarrassed by the ambiguous attitude this Marion de Valdeclare was taking, since the evening was being held in his honor. Trying to smooth things over, he repeated, "He's so mysterious!" with a short laugh.

"How old are you?" the Argentinean asked with some insolence.

"The age when one's voice breaks, anyone can hear that . . . ," Marion replied, looking him straight in the eye. "Seventeen, if you like!"

Midalge cut it short by filling glasses and offering around the biscuits. In the hubbub that followed, the small dark-haired man went up to Marion.

"I feel that from tonight I shall be obsessed with the thought of seeing you again," he whispered. "You are an extraordinary person, Marion de Valdeclare!"

"Well, well, you've remembered my name. I do not know yours."

Midalge bent over and said in a low secretive voice, "He's already crazy about you. Don't be so cruel."

"And am I crazy about him?"

"Who are you crazy about, dear?"

This the others heard.

"No one," Marion declared very loudly.

"You have time!" said Emilio.

"You take me for a young pup, sir. You may be making a big mistake. There is, in any case, an expression which describes me and which has already been applied to me: I care for no one and nothing."

"In that case," Totote exclaimed, "what monstrous cruelty to show your face in public!"

"What a hit!" smirked Midalge.

But Emilio, jealous of the small dark-haired man, and

perhaps also of Totote, threw out treacherously, "At seven-teen one likes to give oneself airs. Perhaps the mystery is simply that Monsieur de Valdeclare is still in high school?"

"Him?" cried Midalge. "But he knows everything, my dear! He's Pico de la Mirandola[2] himself. Why, one of my friends said of him that . . ."

Marion grew impatient. "Let's talk about something else! Say, Midalge, tell us about your latest conquests!"

Julien Midalge pulled a comic face.

"He wants to add to his brood of clear yolks!"

"Precisely."

There was a ripple of laughter. To mark the end of this irksome conversation, the Argentinean asked, "Were you at the Conservatory on Sunday?"

"But of course!" Midalge enthused ecstatically. "Gaubert was sublime."

"I'd give all the concerts in Paris for one mass at Saint-Clothilde!" Totote declared. "Tournemire is quite marvel-ous."

Impassioned and pedantic, they talked music with a series of "quite monstrous!" and "marvelous, marvelous," a few "it has its quaint sides," and many other technical terms.

Marion breathed more easily. Painting would be next, then literature, then all the latest gossip. Lying back on the sofa, surrounded by gold embroidered cushions, he felt comfortable. His pocket was full of cigarettes; he was warm. The familiar impression of being invisible began to invade. The chatter of other people's voices stopped him thinking. It was almost as sweet as nothingness, a kind of sleep illus-trated by human voices and gestures—a moment of oblivion.

But the small dark-haired man kept looking at him in silence, touching in his mute devotion and mesmerized curiosity, an adolescent enthralled by the beginning of a novel for which his imagination alone would pay all the costs. Youth, illusion—the tragedy of youth.

"Poor kid!" thought Marion.

But never once did he bestow upon his victim his asexual gaze. The gaze of an archangel.

Midnight. The cigarettes filled the air with phantasms which floated above their heads, the glasses glistened in their hands, the air was balmy with the scent of flowers. In affected tones which expressed, amid the lies and banter, the occasional real feeling, the gentlemen gathered together that evening had finally begun to talk of love.

[IV]

So the nameless horror of my childhood was an even darker story than the eternal poison its memory has left in my soul.

But could my parents have behaved any differently?

The martyrdom I suffered was only the logical consequence of their own.

I have, unfortunately, spent enough time in the company of that despicable class known as the bourgeoisie to realize what my parents must have suffered, they who considered themselves far superior to the middle class: nobility, in fact, and country nobles at that; feudal lords, in short.

An only son to be the pride and joy of their lives, to continue their name—which was a fine one—and that that son should have been me!

My birth, which of course no one ever told me about,

must have been a scene of unprecedented drama, the registration of that birth a masterpiece of deception, my baptism a lake of tears choked back.

Too late did I recognize my mother's genius. Too late unraveled the clues of her love, or at least the pity she had for me. It was she who found my dual-purpose name, just as she found the means to help me cross the formidable plains of childhood without myself or anyone else discovering what it was that made her lower her eyes, what it was that put me beyond the pale of normal humanity, destined inexorably and as though deservedly to shame and disgrace.

Had my father not been that ferocious squire feared by all around, the narrow jail of my upbringing might perhaps have been alleviated in some way. But that arrogant, judgmental man had the best of reasons to hate me. All he could do not to let his caste down was to keep in check his continual desire to strangle the fairy-tale monster his unhappy wife had brought into the world. I still remember with a shudder how he used to come and look at me in my little bed when I was sick.

During the first years, the hope of having another child— a real son—must have helped him bear his humiliation. But one has to understand that when he realized he would never have another heir, any indulgence, even the simplest gesture of tenderness, became an offense in his eyes. I owe him some gratitude for the fact that he never beat me, nor had me beaten. As a child I lived within hand's reach of my repressed, would-be murderer. All things considered, I have to acknowledge that he treated me like a gentleman. My education was perfect. Since my mind was the only part of me which was not against nature, at least they pulled out all the stops to cultivate that rich ground, even though it would yield no results beyond myself, stricken as I was with sterility.

I think I can reconstruct my unfortunate parents' tragedy pretty well. Thinking everything over, I have discovered all the secrets they kept from me.

My father was handsome, fascinating, and authoritarian when he met my mother. He and his brother, soldiers to the marrow both, played havoc with all the young hearts in their garrison. Inevitably, they were in debt to the eyebrows. Only a prestigious marriage could save their good names, which were in grave jeopardy.

From my aunt's endlessly repeated gossip I got all the details of how they both wanted her for their wife, her and the millions from her family's ironworks. When she chose my uncle, there was an irrevocable rupture between the brothers. They were never to see each other again.

My father's situation became critical. As his creditors began to harass him more and more publicly, he was in danger of being thrown out of the army.

It was at that moment that the frail little English girl, daughter of one of the richest coal merchants in Newcastle, appeared on the horizon. She fell in love with him at first sight, even renouncing her religion so she could marry him.

My grandparents, who died before I was born, were still alive at that point, living in the loathsome *château* (since bombed, thank God), which now belongs to me. (How fitting that I should be the heir—or the heiress—of a ruined castle!)

That poor old couple, mortgaged to the hilt by their sons, must have shed many a tear between those walls no longer standing, those walls where I, their pitiable descendant, endured my long oppressive childhood.

I will never know what ingenious lies my mother told so she could renounce her Protestantism and get married as a Catholic without her family guessing she had repudiated the faith. The marriage must have taken place very quietly in some obscure corner of Paris or the provinces. I only know that my paternal grandparents did everything they could to prevent it, outraged that their eldest son should marry a foreigner, an inveterate Calvinist whose renunciation was a shameful mockery. For in my family, religion came before the family name, it came even before money, which is not without its own nobility, after all.

Nevertheless, my grandparents were crazy about their two sons and nothing could induce them to disinherit my father.

And now I can reveal another side of the drama. I am certain that when I put in my confounding appearance in the world, each of my parents saw me as the just retribution of their respective Gods. Their fanaticism must have been provoked beyond measure, added to their remorse and regrets. I was the very embodiment of the curse of heaven, not to mention my unseemly frailty. My father had never really loved my mother. After I came into the world, he must have loathed her. Did she still adore him? I believe she did, simply remembering how she would blush with embarrassment in his presence.

My poor little mother . . . How I regret never having loved her! That touching loyalty stopped her telling me even of the existence of the bible, which she evidently read every day in secret and which I later inherited. Although she did not go so far as to make her confession before she died, throughout her life she endured the presence of the priest assigned to me and she advised me passionately to go to the Jesuit Seminary. Her love for my father made divorce impossible despite his black moods and the fact that his frequent trips to Paris, as she knew, meant not visits to lawyers as he claimed, but gambling and women, things one does not give up when one has a certain temperament, especially when one's home is nought but a perpetual nightmare. That such a husband should give up his military career to go and bury himself in the northern beet fields was, in her eyes, doubtless a more than sufficient sacrifice.

I, too, forgive my father his infidelities. He had lost hope. Why should he inter the remains of his youth in our grisly *château?* That he spent part of his life there because of me was already pretty commendable.

His only real revenge was to send me to the Jesuits without telling me anything about my physical peculiarity. Not daring to throw me to my death, he threw me to life as soon as he was free of my mother's protective presence. Had she been alive, she never would have let me leave, I am absolutely certain.

Dying as soon as he rejoined his unit at the front, he never felt the need during his illness to call me to him one last time. His hatred must still have been strong.

I think of the ironic satisfaction he must have cherished in his heart as a magnificent revenge throughout the time he knew I was in college, where he could well imagine the method by which my young companions undertook to let me know what kind of phenomenon I was.

Work days, the only days when I truly lived!

I could say, "Work days, the only days when I did not suffer a fate worse than death!"

My brain, the only really masculine part of me, was continually avenging me for the liberties taken and the ill-treatment meted out by my fellow pupils. Always first in every subject, I could justifiably respond to their torments with that crushing superiority which no one could deny.

I far preferred the worst of their cruelty to the sweetest caress. Only God and the director will know all the complicated details of the exploits I provoked at college. They ranged from the coarsest practical jokes to the most passionate rivalry. I don't know whether the humiliations I suffered at that time were greater during the day, when I was insulted by the laughter of the class, or at night, when two fanatic admirers blacked each other's eyes over me.

Certainly my horror of physical coupling was born in the college dormitories. Doubtless, I should thank destiny for having put me off sexuality at such a young age. Whether joy or pain, it comprises the main occupation of men and women. If all the Laurette Wells and all the Julien Midalges whom I know now knew what I really am, one lifetime would not suffice to cultivate all my perversities.

Who knows? Maybe I would be less unhappy? Should I, after all, thank destiny? When I see the quivering interest they all take in it, sometimes I regret being only a brain; that the possibilities given me by nature don't allow me to experience doubly what seems to be their only reason for breathing.

Love, how I hate you, instinct of normality, I who am outside the norm! *Ecce homo! Ecce mulier!*[1] In whichever direction my love goes, I cannot avoid being an invert. I have often envied the fat nurse who used to flirt with the soldier in the park. I envied the soldier as much as I envied her. No one will love me and accept my love as those two love and accept each other. Each time I think *Love,* I will hear the answer *Vice.*

But why was I born with a heart so precise when my sex is so ambiguous?

At first my stay at my uncle and aunt's really seemed like it would be an oasis finally appearing on the horizon in the immense desert of my childhood. I did not know that it was there the supreme indignity awaited.

I was in mourning for my father, I had all my qualifications, degrees[2] as we say in English: Why did I have to be a wretched minor, entrusted by the law into the hands of my father's brother, my enemy, the only person in the family who was responsible for me?

Not having had any children, he and his rich wife pretended to welcome me as a blessing. But the director of the college had notified them, and in any case my perpetual awkward age was already, at the age of nineteen, beginning to give me away.

My slim girlish figure, my fragility, my voice which had not managed to become a man's but which was no longer that of a girl; they had all the proof they needed. Nevertheless, when I left college they found it necessary to have me examined by a doctor.

He declared, despite what was written on my birth certificate, that all things considered it was better to classify me among the female sex. I will never forget the words of that doctor, pronounced in a scientific tone, worse than all the jeers of my classmates.

"Unfortunate individuals like yourself are sometimes lucky enough to grow a beard, you understand. But yours will never grow and that will, in the end, excite suspicion. So it is best to make up your mind while there is still time. You are only nineteen years old, you are not yet known in the world. Cases like yours are not unheard of in the legal domain. It will be easy to have your status rectified at the next meeting of the medical board."

My uncle rubbed his hands with joy. His bitterness toward my father had outlived the man himself. What a fine trick he would play on his memory! That famous son of whom he had been so jealous, without knowing the truth, he was going to make a girl of him—and an old maid at that, since I was unfit for marriage.

In vain did I rebel. My Aunt de Valdeclare took charge of my wardrobe. She was fat and both spineless and stubborn, crammed to the brim with the conventions and prejudices of her kind. Not having any choice but to keep me in her home till I came of age, she took it upon herself to introduce me into her domestic arrangements, albeit with very bad grace. Her husband was all for it and, like my mother, she was afraid of her husband. Seeing me struggle with my feminine attire amused him more than anything else in the world. He went so far as to have someone accompany me the first few times I went out, rejected any garment which was not exclusively feminine, took a fancy for gaudy dresses and stylish hats, ordered me to let my hair grow and made it his duty to present me in the world. He complained continually about my incurable laryngitis. He had retired from the army and was at a loose end; I was his puppet. The enormous joke provided hours of entertainment. I never saw such fierce joy as his the day he was asked for my hand in marriage by a young Master de Forges of his acquaintance. I was believed to be rich, I was known to have a law degree, and although I looked too strange to be considered charming in the kind of world I was entering, I could pass for beautiful.

My aunt's heart was divided between the joys of avarice and a taste for empty luxury. The things I saw among those people turned me emphatically toward the kind of life I live today. I might perhaps have considered it a blessing, for lack of anything better, to establish myself on the side of bourgeois convention. The horrors I witnessed close up for two years, while I was at my uncle and aunt's, gave me a taste for social outlaws, I who should have sought only to avoid them, being outside the law myself.

My first attempts at revolt quietened down into the desolation of permanent demoralization. I did not yet realize that by my double nature I would become a kind of Asmodeus[3] for whom life has at least the attraction of a spectacle complete in all its details, details which are kept well hidden from those who cannot penetrate their mysteries as an unsuspected spy, as I could.

Learning to be a girl was, henceforth, as important for me as all the preparations for the *baccalauréat*.[4]

Meanwhile, I continued to study law. I had the luck, in my misfortune, to be born at a time of sexual confusion. How would I manage now if custom and fashion didn't constantly help me pass from one personality to another without anyone noticing, not even the concierges in my two dwellings?

At twenty-two I was able to leave my guardian and his wife from one day to the next to develop in poverty (how I loved that poverty!) until the day I discovered the scoundrels for whom I now work. I didn't dare resume my masculine garb until much later.

Keeping my name was the best trick I could play on that awful couple who for two years amused themselves so cruelly at my expense, adding unprecedented suffering to that which had already been heaped upon me since birth. They will never dare to give me away. They would have to admit the change my uncle insisted on, and God knows where that whole thing would lead them. Moreover, I move in circles that have never heard of them.

I played other tricks on them, which they will learn of one day, if I decide to make my own confession. My aunt's rich friends, with all their detectives, were never able to put their hands on the mysterious fur thief whose exploits filled the newspapers of the day.

Sensual pleasures are not for me. I have, however, been acquainted with that of skinning the rich dowagers whose homes I was dragged to or sent by force, as a sullen young lady to be married off. Their magnificent stoles, mufflers, sable tippets would disappear as though miraculously, and it would be my dangerous pleasure next day to hear their shrieks at being fleeced, and to read, in the corner by the respectable family radiator, the excited musings of the daily papers.

Who would have thought of looking in my briefcase crammed with student papers, in the antechambers where I would drop it and collect it again later? Who was ever discerning enough to follow me and see what lonely bank I walked along at night and what kind of packages, tied up with string and weighted down with big stones, I threw into the dark waters of the Seine at the end of a winter's day? I regret that I was never able to steal their pearls. But gold snuff boxes, miniatures, and other expensive knickknacks suffered from my occasional bouts of kleptomania to join all the other transportable items I'd been able to fling into the Seine.

When I speak of certain things, or gaze at people with a certain look in my eyes, men and women alike stare at me with the same expression tempered with a kind of fear. They are right. I would scare them even more if they knew what I was thinking about sometimes. I often run the risk—and this pleases me—the risk of letting them guess what I am.

If they were to find out, however, I would be lost once again, when I have more or less found my feet, established an equilibrium, shaky but well-balanced, the equilibrium of my paradoxical life in Paris where so many people know me: superficial Paris, always in a hurry, where no one has the time to go deeply into anything—luckily for me.

But all the same, how much that "unfortunate individual" whose beard will never grow would love to be able to go to bed some night without sighing that little word from his early childhood!

It's so sad: "Bobo, the story of everything! . . ."

[V]

"Finding a publisher," what a dreadful experience. Like that mob standing in the rain behind the bus. The people with numbered seats tried to get on first, their faces declaring implacably, "It's my right." The others crept aboard, hoping to get on under false pretenses as they elbowed each other out of the way.

"Myself, I don't give a damn," thought Marion. "I never take a number."

Standing apart from the scrum, he mused, "How truly splendid to work under someone else's name. No need for a number. My books are published, my plays performed, I earn my crust and no one bothers me."

While the bus was starting up, he climbed calmly on board, the extra passenger clinging to the platform, one of

the little crowd of people standing at the back, packed together like those clumps of human figures you see sometimes
on medieval stained glass windows. And soon variations
on his theme were underscored by harmonies composed of
rhythms produced by the heavy vehicle.

"My renunciation would be ascetic if I weren't alone in
the world. But I have no one to dazzle, for that's what glory
is, the ability to dazzle, which is pretty comical since no one
ever truly amazes anyone else. When it comes down to it,
people are really only interested in themselves. If the audience were made up of Martians, then maybe! But among
human beings . . ."

He lit a cigarette and continued his meditations. When
visiting certain theatre persons, it is a good idea to remember
certain things.

Once, a few years ago, alone in the shadows of the empty
auditorium, had he not seen a famous author and an equally
famous actor nearly come to blows during a rehearsal!

"Excuse me, friend, you are not performing this scene in
the spirit which I intended. I am, after all, the author!"

The actor crossed his arms and called upon his fellow
tragedians as witnesses, "This man's lines are completely
flat!"

Another time an actor in a minor role, not much more
than a walk-on part, whose only business was to say,
"Madam is served," could not get the intonation right.

"You have the delivery of a pig," said the others.

"Don't you worry," he replied. "I save myself for the
dress rehearsal."

And everyone knows Constant Coquelin's response when
he had to wear a false nose to play Napoleon.

"I'll make something of it."

Knowing exactly what angle to take on life as soon as he set foot inside Ginette Lobre's house, Marion pulled the bell cord with the required attitude. Reality was no longer at issue. In the long run most actors stop being bona fide human beings, as though their roles had taken them over like seven demons. At one moment, they act the part of demigods; the next, lousy hams who would have been beaten with cudgels in former days. In order to understand them, without erring too far in one direction or another, one should consider them "ingenuous," which explains their finest qualities and excuses their worst.

It would obviously be hard to live the most intense part of one's life through a pair of opera glasses without ever seeing, even in one's private life, from the "stage perspective," which is no more than a magnifying glass after all. The importance actors assume is not much greater than that which is rightfully theirs, since they are the flesh and bones of a multiplicity of abstractions that, though they have not sprung from their minds, must nevertheless be embodied by their voice and gestures before reaching the public. They are the medium, literally, between the creator and his audience. Consequently they run more risks than the creator, who gives only of his mind, while they give of their whole being.

To go back and forth endlessly between the stage and the wings is to alternate between the purest of ideals and the darkest of daily life. This continual seesaw almost always starts up again once the living puppet has gone back into its box and the play is over.

From the entrance hall Marion could already hear the overly enunciated exclamations of the men and women he had come to see.

Ginette Lobre, the great star of the *Planches modernes,* had a mansion that one entered via a steep staircase leading down to the bear pit she was so proud of, which constituted her main sitting room.

Visitors could be seen from below as they arrived and, from one step to another, could create any effect they pleased.

A series of odd little rooms radiated out from the immense hall, their low ceilings a stark contrast to the dome in the middle. All the furnishings were a mixture of ancient, modern, and exotic; Louis XVI and Directoire blended with Chinese lacquer and creations dreamed up by the boldest of contemporary designers to avoid any hint of the "antiquity corners" of contemporary department stores.

The taste of the stars is unerring nowadays. At Ginette Lobre's one could fancy oneself in the home of a Duchess surrounded by portraits of her ancestors, family furniture, foreign souvenirs, and her latest whimsy, but the illusion was broken by the abundant flower baskets, the incense floating in the air, the fashionable little yap dog, the first names being bandied about, the low divan under the rose colored lights, and especially by the ladies—five or six of them—forming a harem on the cushions of the divan, their backs to the wall, lying stretched out next to each other, a Spanish shawl over their knees as a blanket.

The men are scattered about here and there, opposite this central core, wherever they can find the armchairs and footstools left to them.

"My dear girl" and "What ho, old man!" provide the conversational commas. The accepted style is to appear good-natured, even to the extent of seeming gauche, which in no way impedes the low rumble of backbiting, just like anywhere else—even less than elsewhere.

Marion thought he was simply coming to meet the man whose name appeared on the play he himself had written almost entirely, about some changes Ginette had asked for. He went down the stairs to the bear pit in a bad mood. Tonight, as always, he would figure as no more than a kind of secretary, much needed, but still only a secretary. He was not pleased to find himself in the middle of the little reception. The group ethos required, however, that he be greeted with great effusions.

"Oh, look, it's Mario!"

"Hello there, Mario!"

Ginette rushed over to hug him. Masculine hands were held out.

"My little Mario! How are you doing? . . . I think you know everyone here! Not that it matters! You'll meet them now! This is Mario!"

Those who had never seen him before were amazed and craned their necks to see.

"Goodness!" they said to themselves, believing themselves transfixed. The women, sweet and quite indifferent, curled up against each other, with girlish gestures and excessive make-up, of indeterminate age since there was no authentic thirty-year-old face with which to make a comparison. Their short hair was either curled or plastered down on their foreheads but uniformly dyed or hennaed; their necks were bare; their dresses created by top designers, their jewels of great price. They were making quite a racket on their divan.

"Ninon, you're taking up all the room!"

"Oh, you wretch! You're pushing me off!"

"I say, old chap, that hurt you know."

A journalist took advantage of this childish quarrel to get his hands on their arms and legs.

"I'll make you comfortable! There! . . . Like that everyone has room."

"Now Ginette will recite for us!"

"Go on, Ginette!" Fabrice Maugier, the great actor, called out.

Ginette would not.

"Why don't you recite, dear friend!"

"You know very well I never recite except on stage, my dear!"

Chorus: "Yes, yes . . . Make him recite!"

"Verlaine!"

"No! Baudelaire!"

"No! The Countess de Noailles!"

"I say, old chap, you're not going to make us beg!"

He shook his head. Ginette was practically sitting in his lap.

"Recite for us!"

"Ginette, my dear, you have never looked so beautiful. What eyes! Have you seen her eyes?"

"Just like Semiramis!" declared a flamboyant redhead who had no idea who that queen was.

"I say, old chap, I think you should talk about me! You are so magnificent. Isn't she magnificent?"

"Magnificent," echoed the whole divan.

"She'll recite for us," the journalist announced.

"Yes! Yes! . . . Good idea!"

But two maids brought in tea on trays.

"Who'll be mother?" Ginette asked in the din.

No one answered.

While she poured the tea, Marion came up to her.

"Well? . . . What about the play? . . . The author isn't here? . . . I find a tea party in his place?"

"Oh, my dear, that's right! We forgot to tell you. He's not coming today because . . ."

"I want some of those cakes over there!"

"Ginette, sugar!"

"Mario, give me one of your cigarettes."

"Who'll recite for us, then?"

"Have you heard Tholomas's latest?"

"No! Do tell! Do tell!"

While malicious gossip spread through the room in the thin smoke of the cigarettes, Marion, standing quite apart, watched as an awkward, inelegant young man who had not yet said a word came timidly toward him, clutching his tea cup clumsily.

"Monsieur," he said softly, "I understand from what you were just saying to Madame Lobre that you collaborated on a play she is rehearsing . . . Well . . . I'm not at all up on things . . . I come from the provinces . . . Everyone tells me I have talent . . . I've written a three-act play . . . My manuscript keeps being sent back to me, when it is sent back! . . . I mean, it keeps being rejected. Sometimes people invite me to things, like today, I don't know why . . . Well . . . I assure you, I have talent . . ."

"Talent?"

Standing in the doorframe of one of the little rooms, Marion drank his tea thinking that pretty soon he would be off.

"You think it helps, having talent, when you're trying to get your plays performed?"

"What?" said the other, dropping his spoon.

"To get performed in Paris, at least on the *Planches modernes,* if you don't already have a name, you need two things. Do you have them?"

"What things?"

Marion put down his empty cup and lit a cigarette.

"Money and a whore."

Laughter at the Tholomas's story covered everything. Marion turned on his heels.

"Where are you going, Mario?"

Ginette caught up with him at the bottom of the stairs.

"Oh, my dear, you can't leave before I've had time to talk to you. A marvelous scheme with . . ."

"Ginette, recite for us!"

"Say, let Marion recite for you!"

Amidst the great jeers of laughter provoked by these words, Fabrice Maugier threw himself on Ginette so he could carry her off by force to face her public. She responded by slapping his hands. They fought with each other while at the same time kissing each other on the mouth. Marion, shoved aside in the fray, found himself next to the shy young man.

"By the way, Monsieur, do you know what 'a scheme' is?"

"No . . . ," he replied, wide-eyed.

"Well, you need to know that before you waste time writing plays. It's the art of theatre nowadays. Without a scheme you are no more than the bloody author—in other words, you're nothing."

At the other end of the hall a voice straight out of the conservatory pierced the henhouse cackle.

"Ginette has always been a great idealist!"

Marion had pricked up his ears.

"Educate yourself, Monsieur! You need only listen to

what people say. One learns theatre work as one would a foreign language taught by the Berlitz method. Ginette the idealist, translates as not one, not two, not three, but a whole syndicate of useful lovers. Over in our corner, you and I are the superfluous ingredients at this reception; no one will even notice we're listening."

"But Monsieur . . . ," the young man murmured.

Ginette's voice, suddenly authoritative, asserted, "A good play? Believe you me! The maximum every night! Yesterday we made twelve thousand!"

"There you have theatrical criticism, Monsieur . . . ," Marion went on coldly.

Without even bothering to keep his voice down, "One cannot attach the same meaning to the word 'play' as did our worthy predecessors. Theatre today, you understand— except of course for the exception which proves the rule—is a branch of the Stock Exchange. If you want your percentage back, you have to invest a little beforehand, don't you?"

"Are you trying to tell me that, as an author, more is required of me than my play?"

"Unless you collaborate with a well-known name, who'll take all the glory for himself, without having written a single word, naturally . . . if you're lucky enough that your name doesn't get dropped en route! Take it or leave it. Scheme, Monsieur, scheme. That's the motto of our era in every field. Sometimes a good cast of the net picks up the whole shoal of rotten fish [1] in one go. But that only happens in banking."

"You're very demoralizing, Monsieur!"

"Keep your illusions, Monsieur! I ask nothing better. But you'll keep your play along with them."

"Monsieur . . . Won't you read it for me?"

Marion swallowed back his laugh as soon as it came out with that terrible hiccuping sound. The young man stepped back, no doubt startled, no doubt offended, no doubt transfixed by this young pup with the eunuch's voice, who was nothing more than a peevish little failure. A moment later he had gone, his absence no more noticeable than his presence.

Marion came back and sat down on the side by the divan. He examined the women with the attentive scrutiny of a former kleptomaniac. No. He had no desire to rob them. They were what they were without shame, and their lives were made up of struggles of all kinds, all kinds of courage. They were well acquainted with hard, conscientious work, simple good heartedness, and even a certain lyricism. The magnifying glass would show other things besides vanity, venality, wigs, and false noses. It would see the birth and development of many talents, sometimes even of genius.

"When one is part of a commercial enterprise," he concluded, "it's a fine thing to trade in wild fancies. On stage all these people express a genuinely-felt emotion."

"Recite some poetry for us!"

It was no longer possible even to tell who was being addressed.

Marion felt a touch on his arm.

"I say," whispered the journalist, "It seems you know Laurette Wells, eh?"

He gave a lewd wink.

"Will you take me there some day?"

Marion did not even bat an eyelid as he replied, "I'm afraid you're mistaken, my friend. I don't know her."

"Oh? . . . What a pity!"

The little dog yapped, adding to the racket. A new arrival appeared at the top of the stairs, made a graceful descent, hugged everybody, called everyone "tu," and took her place on the divan. Yet again Marion heard voices demanding from the wings, "Who'll recite for us?" and without anyone making a move to detain him, even Ginette, who had such an important matter to discuss, he went off without saying goodbye.

It was still raining. Behind the bus the little scuffle was starting again. Marion mused to himself that the word "foule" (crowd) was truly the feminine of "fou" (mad)[2] and decided to take a taxi. He nodded to himself behind the rattling cab window, "At Laurette's or Midalge's house, one talks art, music, even love with respect and ceremony. Beauty and money are never discussed in the same sentence. For dirty perverts, they are decidedly clean-minded. While that other fellow, that journalist, who looks like a traveling salesman on a spree, imagined Laurette's home to be a house of ill repute. I'd like to see him at one of her salons, attending a string quartet or forced to listen to the poetry reading these professionals have been unable to put on!"

His sick laugh made him ill. A thought struck him. Knocking on the window in front, Marion quickly gave the driver a new address.

[VI]

A little rest after weeks of work, that's what Marion was looking for in her apartment in the 16th. No work in progress lay waiting to tempt her male and female imagination. There were no real books there, no piles of papers, no work table calling to her. The delicate secretaire in the living room was only good for writing a letter or two. Here it would not have been fitting to contemplate more than putting flowers in vases, reading the latest novels to keep oneself up to date, writing out the list of feminine purchases to be made in the shops, dreaming about a new suit, shoes, silk stockings, going for a stroll, warming oneself upon one's return from shopping, planning a visit to Laurette . . .

Oddly enough, while she was looking over her apartment—small living room, bedroom, kitchen—Miss Hervin

discovered a letter from Laurette on her secretaire, surrounded by a pile of handbills. As usual, Laurette had not
failed to write the most important part of her message on the
envelope, "Better make it Thursday for lunch, at my house,
with Janine and two other women who are coming over
specially to meet you."

"Oh terrific! . . . " the breaking voice grumbled. "Today's
Friday."

Marion unsealed the envelope and spent five minutes trying to understand both the handwriting and the import of
the letter, in which everything doubled back and contra-
dicted itself. As always, she ended up abandoning the crazy
little note. No explanation, either written or verbal, would
follow moreover. Laurette never seriously believed in the
rendez-vous she set up.

Miss Hervin sighed. She took out a cigarette and filled her
inner emptiness with new spirit as she inhaled the zigzags of
smoke. An unreliable companionship, that dance of the ge-
nies of the air.

Cushions scattered on the little sofa, some silk, some gold,
a rather fine rug, some family furniture, a bookcase laden
with hand-sewn books: This little nook at the top of the
characterless modern house was welcoming and well put-
together. The electricity gave a steady, cheerful light, the
radiators warmed the room, and behind the closed velvet
curtains the windows looked out onto a neat courtyard and
a row of rooftops beyond which one could see as far as Passy
and even a few trees.

Miss Hervin stretched out on her sofa the better to savor
the cigarette in the light of the low lamp, the only one

she'd left on. A distant hum rolled like a wave over Paris, ceaseless, oceanic.

Forcing oneself not to think would have been an impossible task without a cigarette, that all-purpose good fairy. For smoking provides assistance in every circumstance of life. If one is alone, one is less alone; if one is in cheerful company, one is more cheerful yet; if one is bored with people, one is not so bored; if one is searching for ideas, one finds them the more easily; if one is waiting, if one is anxious, if one is idle, if one is working, a cigarette, that intoxicant, that habit, is indispensable. It has neither the same taste nor the same significance, but varies according to place, mood, and moment. This vice, which seems so monotonous to others, is perhaps the most varied there is.

"To be able to smoke when one wants," Marion mused, "is a small enough pleasure, but not to smoke would be a great misfortune. When one looks closely, one is not really sure one likes that bitterness in the mouth, but one knows it would be unbearable to do without it. Do we not judge the importance of a thing, and even of an emotion, most of all by its lack?"

As a sleeper slips unconsciously into a dream, Miss Hervin, without noticing, was slipping back into her habitual sadness. The poor soul was thinking that in her solitary existence, an animal would have brought comfort. But a cat would spend long days uncared for in the empty apartment, a dog could not be both Marion's companion and, at the same time, Mario's. That would inevitably give the secret away.

"So it's precisely because I am two that I must always be

a woman alone, or a man alone. Why, why didn't my mother follow the instinct of her womb to its rightful conclusion and make me the boy and girl I should have been? How we would have loved each other! Telescoped one into the other, we are too many for a single being, or rather, we are nothing at all . . ."

She tried to feel her twin at her side—the phantom of her childhood. But now she *knew* and the fantasy was over.

She straightened up to lean on her elbows, flattening the thin bust which from the first glance labeled her English. A second cigarette accompanied her thought.

"Supposing I had a weak heart, I could die on this sofa, just like that . . . Madame Creponnet, the concierge, would be extremely alarmed when she climbed the stairs soon after to prepare dinner; then she would be extremely put out. As for me, it would be as though everyone were dead since I would no longer exist . . ."

The long hand stretched out along the cheek which cradled it.

"Isn't it already as though everyone else were dead, ever since my birth, since I'm not human as others are? I love no one, have never loved anyone, will probably never love anyone. Nothing will make me believe I have the right even to love an animal. When I die, my death will be a catastrophe for myself alone, if one believes death is a catastrophe. If someone loved me, I would feel responsible for the beating of another heart, and then I would be precious in my own eyes, and I would defend myself against death. But no one needs me emotionally. I am the center of no magnificent egotism. And because no one would cry if I died, I sometimes cry for myself, the only mourning there will be for me."

Dwelling on such thoughts takes up more time than one thinks. When the cigarette was finished, the thin fingers threw what was left in the ashtray, then lingered a while suspended in empty space. The pupils grew larger, blue and bathed in shadow.

"Will no one ever come?"

"It's me, Mam'zelle Hervin!" the concierge cried out comically as she came in through the kitchen.

"Oh, is that you, Madame Creponnet?"

Marion's laughter was smothered in a corner of the cushion, in the exact spot where her sobs were to have been muffled.

She had had to remain Miss Hervin until the end of the law examination, which she'd started in a frock, then revert to young Valdeclare in order to collaborate anonymously with famous authors on the wane. By disappearing from femininity, Marion rid herself of several flirts who had been edging too close to her threadbare secretary skirts. Nowadays this alternative was useful in her life spent fleeing the world, and helped her gain entry into the only social set which interested her.

Friendly feelings for Laurette warmed her heart a little as she returned to the sofa after dinner.

"I'll go and see her tomorrow . . . ," she decided.

And, to put an end to her efforts at reading her own destiny, she dived halfheartedly into the latest insipid novel "hot off the press."

Laurette had not yet gone out and appeared charmed by the visit. She was wearing boots under her suit, but nevertheless complained of having cold feet. After a while she began to pace the room, her back even straighter than usual, her eyes stern.

"Marion," she said, "since you're here, you will have to help me."

"Most flattered by your confidence, Laurette! How may I be of service?"

"One of the girls who came to lunch on Thursday occasionally visits with Aimée de Lagres, the one I made divorce her husband."

"Oh yes! . . . and whom you left four months later?"

"Yes, Marion. It seems she is consoling herself with the old Countess Talliard, and that I cannot bear. She must be torn free from the clutches of that banal giraffe. She dishonors me. I cannot accept such a successor."

"But what if she's happy?"

"Happiness is of no consequence. I prefer to take her back."

"It will mean certain heartache for her."

"Marion, she is worthy of being made to suffer. She is a very rare little creature. And her ankles are as slender as a doe's, and such beautiful hands! And melancholy eyes with a little pursed mouth. Such a pretty thing . . ."

"In a word, you miss her!"

Laurette stopped her pacing.

"I would like her to have someone like you. But I know how you are . . ."

"So you're sacrificing yourself."

Laurette sat down so she could give full vent to laughter. Hers was the laugh of a fourteen-year-old girl. Then she gazed at Marion with the look she had when someone saw through her, shame and complicity both. Her listless voice spoke hurriedly, her eyes looked away, embarrassed to show their animation.

"Since you've met her several times at my house it will seem perfectly natural for you to go and see her. You can say you've come to interview her."

Marion bit back her mirth.

"But for one thing, I'm no longer a journalist, and for another, she hasn't done anything worthy of an interview. She's just another society woman among so many thousand others."

"Can one not interview whomever one likes?"

"No, you silly goose, one cannot."

"Oh well, you'll think of something else. You'll have to arrange to be alone with her, for old Talliard will not leave her side, and you'll tell her I still love her, which is true. I can't do a thing myself because Talliard hates me. I'd also like you to take her twenty-four red roses and twelve arum lilies, which I'll give you."

"That'll be sure to make an impression on the household!"

"Marion, you must do it. I'm very cross with that young lady. She refuses to see me under any circumstance and I want her to come back to me."

Miss Hervin watched the slight tremor which shook Laurette's head.

"You've got your captain's face on, the day of the mutiny on ship. Not a good sign."

"Not good at all," Laurette replied somberly.

"But your battle plan is simply absurd. Why don't you send that other girl who sees Aimée de Lagres from time to time?"

A short scornful laugh accompanied Laurette's shrug.

"She would spoil everything. She's an idiot. You're the only one who could do it successfully."

"I'll be happy to try, but not the way you suggest. The interview, the red roses, the arum lilies, that's all idle fancy."

"Fine, Marion. I'll take the flowers to her myself then. She'll know where they came from. They were her favorites."

It was Marion's turn to shrug.

"The complications of your idle lives amuse me. You make up little stories for yourselves, you make a toy of love. At heart you're just a bunch of schoolgirls—dangerous schoolgirls, moreover, because somewhere in all this is a man who loved his wife and who has lost her, a woman quietly living her life now launched on illicit affairs."

"It was *before* that she was illicit."

Laurette's murmur was almost imperceptible. She nearly always spoke for herself without caring whether anyone else heard or not. She began to pace about the room again and gazed out the windows.

"Yes, I know," said Marion. "You have to go out. Goodbye."

"Come with me, Marion. The carriage will take you wherever you want afterwards. I'm just going over to Margaret Watson's."

"Another new conquest?"

"So pale with that red hair . . . ," Laurette mused aloud as she rang for her chambermaid, "and still doesn't know if she wants to . . ."

[VII]

"Now here I am caught up in other people's immorality," Miss Hervin said to herself when she got back home. "What a fine pursuit for my little vacation!"

Elbow on knee, chin in hand, cigarette in mouth, she amused herself thinking up ways to approach Madame de Lagres until it was time for bed. "Not that it will do any good," she decided, but it was more fun than reading a novel.

She should have been passionate about the cause, loathe the countess-giraffe, imagine that bringing the escapee back into the grasp of Laurette's pink fingernails was a noble act of liberation. Maybe then inspiration would have descended to point out the right path to follow.

What pretext should she invent?

Sleep came before inspiration.

"To sleep . . . like everyone else. All night long to be like any other being . . . What a pity that it takes place in the unconscious."

On the pillow, in that ivory profile, an eye remained open a long time, a blue eye in its delicate cavern, the setting for a beautiful precious stone. The desolate mouth tried to smile. The hair, a disheveled helmet, snaked over the white linen like a band of little reptiles.

One finds miracles in the most banal of sayings, as long as one does not have to put it to the test oneself.

"Night brings counsel, how true that is!" Marion was still chewing the matter over as she made her toilette. Like a scene in a play, without racking her brain any further, she had found the only way to gain entry to the Countess Talliard's house. When she woke up, the plan had made itself.

For the next two days, as she strolled along the local streets, or while she was out shopping, she polished off the fine points of her plan. An old habit of the dramatist. But how much more breathtaking it is to live out a drama than to write one!

On the third day, growing impatient, she paid a morning call at Laurette's so as to be sure not to miss her. It was hardly the customary thing to do, but she was sure she would be welcome all the same.

Once she'd crossed the cold Neuilly garden, she had but a moment to wait in the big downstairs living room.

"Would Mademoiselle like to step upstairs?"

The pedicurist was sitting at the bedside, holding one of

Laurette's ravishing feet in her hand. While she polished the pink shells encrusted on the slender toes, she related all kinds of gossip—secrets and scandals she had unearthed in the houses where she worked. Lying nonchalantly back among the snowdrifts of her bed, Laurette was not even listening. This chatter was part of the job and did not in the least put her off her morose reverie, "Well, Marion? What news? Did you see her?" [1]

And the dialogue continued in French without even a handshake.

"Have I seen her? Laurette, are you serious? I've come to tell you my idea, that's all."

"Oh! I see!" said Laurette in disappointment.

She sat Marion down beside the bed, opposite the pedicurist.

"I went over there early in the morning, the day before yesterday, to lay my roses and lilies at the front door like I told you. In the evening I went back to see if the flowers had been taken away. They were still there, suffering from lack of water. So I brought them home again. There they are. No point making them wretched, is there? You can take them with you when you go. But I've thought of something better to do. I'm going to go and play my violin in the courtyard. Aimée will recognize my tunes. She'll know it's me. I only agreed to learn the violin when I was little because of a vague instinct which told me I would be serenading under windows when I grew up. This won't be the first time either . . ."

"Nonsense," [2] Marion interrupted. "You get more and more practical don't you? Listen! And try and answer without mixing everything up. I believe I remember that Talliard is very fond of rare editions, isn't that so?"

Laurette's eyes glittered suddenly. She guessed the idea before she heard the rest.

"Yes!" she said. "That's just what we needed. You are brilliant, Marion!"

"Wait a moment! I won't be so silly as to turn up with my books (and I have some extraordinary ones, you know!) while Talliard is there! I'll pretend to arrive unexpectedly as though I needed money urgently. But I will have checked out the surrounding area beforehand and made sure that for once Talliard has gone out without her companion. Once sure of finding Aimée alone, you see, it will be easy for me to tell her what you want her to know. And then I will have done my job. But you must give me time to do the thing properly and not start some foolishness of your own in the meantime, which will spoil everything."

"Very good, Marion . . ."

Laurette agreed to everything with humility and confidence, sure of her success in advance as always, whatever the occasion, even when the project was entirely fantastic, and despite both her experience and her skepticism, since she had in her blood the prodigious American optimism.

On the other side of the bed, avid and powerless, the hired hand went on rubbing the same nail for far too long, trying, despite all probability, to catch the drift of this English conversation. She would so much have liked to be able to repeat it elsewhere.

"Marion, you can have my carriage all day to watch the Countess's house."

"What a good idea! That way I would be sure to remain incognito. Your carriage is entirely unknown to those ladies, isn't it?"

"That's true, Marion. I didn't think . . . Then how will you go about it?"

"Leave that up to me. I ask you only to stay out of it."

Once again Laurette murmured, "Very good, Marion."

Certainly no one could have uttered that little word with such calm obedience.

An hour later Marion, laden with flowers, was returning home having refused Laurette's invitation. Before making her first move, she needed to collect her thoughts far from Miss Wells's bewildering utopias.

For a week, a slim young man, a disquieting figure, watched that old block of flats on the embankment. He would sit on a bench on the sidewalk opposite, or dally over a book he was reading at one of the *bouquiniste*[3] stalls. In another area it would have been far harder for him to learn so quickly that the Countess Talliard went out every day from two to three, alone, on foot, holding an Aberdeen terrier on a leash, which she would take for a walk with complete regularity— whether for the animal's health, or for her own, was not recorded.

Madame de Lagres must have been lazy—or tired. Clearly she was not fond of walking. For at five o'clock most precisely Talliard's car would appear and wait in front of the door for the two ladies.

On this particular day, Miss Hervin rang the bell at ten past two. Hidden in her taxi in front of the nearest antique shop, she had just seen the Countess and the dog disappear into the distance.

As she climbed the stairs to the second floor she had had

to slow down, afflicted with heart palpitations. Her burden of books was heavy, composed as it was of precious volumes from her Franciscan library.

"Who knows whether she'll see me? And if she does see me, what kind of figure will I cut offering my books like a pauper? Aimée de Lagres has only met me a couple of times at Laurette's. If she remembers, she will dismiss me immediately, smelling a trap; if she doesn't recognize me, she'll wonder where on earth I've come from and how I know the Countess likes rare books . . . If it comes to that, I have my reply ready, but all the same . . . Why did I get involved in this affair? . . . Come on, don't be a coward! I wanted to have fun, that's all. Whatever happens I'm curious to see how it will all turn out."

A manservant opened the door.

"I would like to see the Countess Talliard . . . ," Marion said very calmly, thinking at the same time, "This is it! The farce has begun!"

"The Countess has gone out, Madame."

"Is there no one I could speak to? I have some old books that she's interested in and I won't be able to come back another time."

The servant must have been familiar with the crazes of the house. He seemed to hesitate, then murmured: "I'll go and see . . . "

As soon as she was alone in the vestibule, a sudden panic seized hold of Marion. She was moving her hand toward the front door when the inside door opened. Madame de Lagres appeared. She blinked for no more than a second.

"Oh! Miss Hervin! Do come in!"

Pale and amazed, and heavily encumbered by her packet

of books, Marion shook the hand held out to her. Good Lord, how simple everything was!

The salon she was shown into was modern and opulent, dry and refined, full of rare little watercolors, shiny black furniture, cubist canvasses, and misshapen lampshades. Despite its bare windows the room remained dark—fortunately for the visitor, since the feeling that she was a traitor had given a very odd cast to her face.

Aimée de Lagres went swiftly over to the lowest of the sofas where she must have been reading the book thrown down among the golden cushions. Miss Hervin got the impression that the pretty little thing was bored, doubtless isolated, and that she was very happy to receive an unexpected visit.

Once they were sitting down, she said, "They say you have some books for Madame Talliard? Does she know about them? Show me!"

Suddenly Marion regained all her sangfroid.

"Do you remember where we met before?" she asked.

"Of course! At Miss Wells's house!"

"Oh! . . . Well, then let me tell you the truth right away. I didn't come about the books. But about something else."

"Oh? . . . And what's that? . . ."

A trace of emotion, a slight blush, a certain brightness of the eye lit up Madame de Lagres's face. Marion felt instinctively that she was ready for adventure, any adventure, provided it broke the monotony of her life. She had time to muse, "Lord, how funny! . . . Even an affair like theirs can become bourgeois!"

"I came on behalf of the woman you just mentioned: Miss Wells . . . She . . ."

"Oh! Her!" the young woman exclaimed, backing away.

"She still loves you!" Marion said hurriedly. "You don't know what a state she's in because of you!"

The other woman burst out laughing with complete insincerity.

"I like that!"

Her hands clawed the nearest cushion.

"You can tell her from me that she will never see me again. Never! Never, do you hear me! I should have suspected something. The other day she left her ridiculous flowers at my door. They've been stolen, what's more! Because I didn't take them. I've had enough of Laurette and her amateur theatricals! I don't even hate her. I consider her unworthy of my attention, that's all. What's got into her now! Why can't she leave me in peace!"

She shrugged violently.

"What a ham that girl is!"

Marion had got to her feet.

"Very good!" she said coldly.

Aimée curled round on the sofa provocatively.

"On no! It's not your fault. Stay a while! I always wanted to get to know you better. Just because Laurette's a . . ."

She practically lowered her voice, "Madame Talliard won't be back for another three quarters of an hour. So why don't you come and sit here . . ."

Her throat swollen with muted laughter, Marion was unable to speak for a few seconds. She regained her self-control, thrust the large package under her arm, and held out her hand.

"My dear Madame, you are charming, but I cannot stay any longer. I had only come to talk about Laurette."

Madame de Lagres did not catch her insolence.

"Bah! What an uninteresting subject! Well, since you're in such a hurry today, you will come back another time, won't you? You'll always find me alone at this time . . . Madame Talliard is walking her dog . . ."

The imperceptible mockery which punctuated this last word caught Marion's attention. What's more, Aimée de Lagres finished off, "Supposing she comes home while you're here, you can still talk about the books then, can't you?"

But on the doorstep, where she was still trying to keep Marion from leaving, she added, "I will never leave the Countess. She's an absolutely perfect friend. She was so good to me when I was ready to kill myself because of Miss Wells (how stupid can you get!). Sorry! You're her friend. But it won't last! But that wouldn't stop us seeing each other from time to time . . . You are so interesting! I don't know anyone like you . . . Well, goodbye! Thanks for coming, all the same. You will come back? Promise? Between two and three, don't forget! I won't tell the Countess you came today. What use would that be? So if you meet her some day by chance . . . Understood? Good. Goodbye! Goodbye, dear Miss Hervin!"

[VIII]

Marion was careful not to let Laurette know of little Miss de Lagres's flirtatious behavior toward her. With her mulish stubbornness, the demented woman would have tormented her for months, maybe years, until Marion became the instrument of Aimée's liberation.

More than a week had passed since Marion's last visit to Neuilly. Laurette made no special commotion when she saw Miss Hervin, for that was not her way; instead, certain of victory, she waited to be told the story of the great battle.

This Marion understood from the expression on Laurette's face, despite her iron self-control. She surprised Laurette writing letters at her desk in the little salon.

"It's not good news . . . ," the hoarse voice murmured.

"You haven't seen her? You weren't able to . . ."

"Oh yes, I saw her."

"Oh! Marion! You are wonderful! But you weren't able to speak to her? Talliard was there?"

"No, not at all! Aimée was alone, I spoke with her at leisure."

"Marvelous! However did you manage it?"

Laurette's eyes sparkled.

"I'll tell you presently. But you should know right away that she will never leave the Countess, she is happy with her and will never see you again under any pretext."

Laurette's short scornful laugh was accompanied by the usual shrug of the shoulders, and the simultaneous raising of her left eyebrow, a sure sign of emotion.

"Fine," she snapped. "We'll think of something else."

"What do you mean 'something else'? The issue does not appear to be in doubt."

Laurette turned away, stiff-backed and full of scorn.

"You just didn't go about it the right way!"

Miss Hervin was not surprised by such injustice and in-gratitude. She had long been familiar with Laurette's bad temper, having often been present at the discomfiture of others.

Patient and somewhat amused, Marion told Laurette of the week she had spent casing the area, then recounted the visit in all its details, saving only those which she wished to keep quiet, and these she passed over in silence.

Laurette listened aggressively.

"That's not what you should have said . . . ," she concluded with an injured look.

"So you think if I had said something different, Aimée's

feelings would have completely turned around? You think people's minds are changed by a few short words?"

"With a little shrewdness, you could have . . ."

Marion sensed that Laurette could go on for hours, days, months. She knew Laurette's powers of recrimination only too well. To cut it short, she got to her feet.

"Goodbye, Laurette!"

"Stay for dinner," said Laurette imperiously. "There's a man coming tonight, Lord Hampton, whom you've already met. The one who's been wanting to marry me for years."

"And who would often quite like to beat you, for your temper and your morals of which he thoroughly disapproves . . ."

"Yes, but he loves me. He could easily be persuaded to do something for me. We're going to use him to get Aimée back."

"You think Madame de Lagres is susceptible to falling for him?"

"Of course not, Marion!" exclaimed Laurette irritably. "Madame de Lagres is incapable of loving a man. That's not it. I had a plan of my own, in case you didn't succeed—which is how it turned out, naturally. I have the whole thing worked out."

"Really? . . . What's the plan?"

"The three of us are going to abduct Aimée."

"Well! Well! And how, exactly?"

"You'll go back and see her again and you'll invite her to go for a little walk with you. My car will be waiting downstairs. Cecil Hampton and I will be in it. At the gate you'll give Aimée a quick push. Cecil will take hold of her, you'll get in behind, and . . . (here she snapped her fingers in that American way which can mean so many different things) the car drives off at top speed."

"Where to, Laurette?"

"To Austria. Princess Margit, whom you've also met, has a *château* in the mountains. She'll lend me it to keep Aimée locked up."

"Fine. But don't you think Aimée will scream out the window for help? And in the middle of a traffic jam, as we're driving through Paris, that might be a little risky."

"Well, of course, Marion! (Laurette's tone said, "Good Lord, how slow you are!") . . . But I've thought of that. We'll inject Aimée with morphine to keep her quiet as long as necessary."

"Oh? . . . Just like that, in the car?"

"Certainly! Cecil will have the syringe all ready."

"And you think Aimée will let herself be injected?"

"Well, as soon as we set off, you'll cry out as though there had been an accident. At that moment, Lord Hampton will inject Aimée. Aimée will exclaim, 'Oh! An accident! Oh! What's pricking me!' and she'll fall asleep."

"And there we are!" Marion finished, straight-faced.

Laurette stared at her, quivering with disapproval, ready to start the same reproaches as before, with no sense that the plans she had outlined were anything other than perfectly natural.

"Are you staying to dinner?" she asked in severe tones.

"Why of course, Laurette! I want to be part of the abduction party, don't you know!"

"We'll go over the fine detail with Cecil. Oh! That's him now!"

For the next two weeks Marion was to derive enormous amusement from this story, beginning with Lord Hampton's rage at the dinner table and again later in the evening. His desire to hit Laurette was so strong that in the end he thought it best to leave, slamming the door behind him, as he had done many a time before in his life, which meant he would go on being angry for a full year.

Miss Wells's plan was consequently in need of modification, but not as much as one might have supposed. The flight into Austria remained on the horizon and Laurette felt no need to let Princess Margit know of her intentions. The Princess would find it perfectly normal to see the abductee and her escort arrive on her mountainside, and would not fail to offer her *château* to imprison the young woman.

During those two weeks, the little apartment in the sixteenth was besieged with letters, telegrams, and messages from Laurette, who refused to have a telephone installed. Miss Hervin continued good-naturedly to play her part in the buffoonery.

In the meantime, Laurette's temper became more and more unbearable. This was her way of expressing unhappiness. Every second day she took to her bed. Seeing Aimée de Lagres again became an almost dangerous obsession. Muffled up in her ermine counterpane, steely-eyed, she performed quite a ritual of romantic mourning around this sorrow, which she had invented out of thin air and in which she ended up believing to the point of giving herself an attack of neurasthenia. Her choir of favorites suffered a thousand snubs and indignities; to the servants, she was a tyrant.

One day when she went into Laurette's bedroom, Marion found the woman lying stretched out on the bed and so pale she was frightened for her. But as she bent down to talk to Laurette more persuasively, she discovered that the rougeless cheeks had been dusted with white powder, instead of the usual pink. Marion glanced round. She noticed the curtains that had been put up at the windows, green curtains which threw a cadaverous light over Laurette's face.

Farce and sincerity, the very soul of Miss Wells was revealed in this stage setting.

"For she must weep when no one is there. The other day her eyelids were really red, despite everything she had put on to hide it . . ."

Generously, Marion did not let it be seen that she had noticed. She listened with resignation to the weak voice as, once again, it scolded, going over and over the same old thing and inventing bizarre schemes . . .

"And to think that if Madame de Lagres had my address, she would write and ask me to come and see her behind the Countess's back! If Laurette only knew!"

Marion kept her secret without compunction. The Laurette for whom she felt a certain sympathy was not the one before her today.

In the end she grew tired of the endless trivia of this sterile affair, born of idleness, wealth, and too many novels. She'd been listening to the same old story for rather too long. Her work called out to her from her bachelor flat on the left bank. One day, without explanation, Miss Hervin disappeared.

After he got to his lowly dwelling with its mosaic of rare books, young Valdeclare had a pretty considerable pile of mail to wade through, sighing as he read, before he could take up his various labors and resume the role of what the theatre world calls "the ghost writer"[1] (that is the one who writes the plays by great authors to which he can never sign his name). There were telegrams, to which he had naturally not replied, ten urgent rendez-vous already out-of-date, two new projects from his usual slave-drivers, a coaxing letter from Ginette Lobre in need of his intellectual lights, a pressing invitation from Julien Midalge to a costume party which had come and gone, cards announcing exhibitions and concerts, a plea from the young author from the provinces asking for his support, two notes from a lawyer asking him to be his secretary, and lastly, the only sentimental item among so much imperious and soliciting paperwork, a passionate letter written by the little dark-haired man he had met at Midalge's house, who had finally discovered his address after feverish searching. Adolescence, fervor and pomposity: it made Marion smile, with a pity not unmixed with a certain tenderness.

[IX]

DECEMBER 17

I wandered along the banks of the Seine, in the rain the asphalt was as reflective as a river. The toing and froing of the cars, trams, and buses seemed like the movement of ships. The lights came on and the illusion was complete. In the twilight, Notre-Dame hulked like a dark ship at anchor. A lost passerby, I followed where my footsteps led me, weary of work, anonymous, sexless, without destination or destiny. My heart was sucked by the leeches of despair. I saw Laurette get out of her car near the house where Aimée lives. She was alone, performing solely for herself, a performance which had caused her a dangerous loss of weight and color since I had last seen her, ten days before.

It is difficult to recognize another person's pain when there is nothing about it which reminds you of your own. Laurette was suffering, and because her suffering would not have been one for me, I could not take her heartache seriously. Her heartache was an effect. One should never trouble oneself with causes.

Remorse at abandoning Laurette roused me from my own sadness. As long as one can do something for others, one is not entirely wretched. I would go and see Laurette presently and put myself once again at her disposal. The whole affair was pitiful, but it was the only opportunity I had to be of use to someone, outside of the work for which I was paid.

I went and hid in a carriage entrance so that Laurette's eagle eye should not pick me out in the crowd. She would immediately have detected Miss Hervin beneath the apparel of young Valdeclare. What a scandal! Within the week the whole of Paris would have known my secret!

Once the danger was over I went back home. I was less wretched. I put a little heart into my work.

DECEMBER 18

I haven't been over to Laurette's yet as I have to finish this act and deliver it before becoming a woman again. In any case, it's about time I went back to Passy. The little dark-haired man from Midalge's is by now writing to me every two days. Last week he came asking for me. The concierge followed my orders. She didn't let him come up. But one of these mornings or one of these evenings I won't be able to help finding myself face to face with him and then there'll be a new Laurette-Aimée affair, translated into the masculine. I'm tired of abnormality. But, since I myself am an anomaly, how can I avoid it? Wherever I go, it will be my lot. There is no one for me on this earth, unless I engage in vice—which I find disgusting and which bores me into the bargain.

DECEMBER 19

I will take advantage of the Christmas holidays. My concierge on the left bank will think I am leaving for London as I tell her each time I disappear. For the concierge at Passy, on the other hand, I will be arriving from London.

Christmas and the New Year are especially loathsome to me. I will not even have the ball and the little clockwork car that were given to me when I was little. There is nothing more ludicrous than the greetings, gifts, and candies exchanged at this time of year. And yet I would like to give and receive some like everyone else. Being outside the rhythm of life, that's my tragedy. Other people's joyful bustle only confirms it the more. When I walk past shops already displaying Christmas trees and sugar tops, I look away with a terrible urge to cry.

Bobo, the story of the holidays . . .

DECEMBER 21

As of this morning I am Miss Hervin once again. I'll go and see Laurette in a moment.

THAT EVENING

Laurette wasn't there. I left a note saying I'd be coming tomorrow.

DECEMBER 22

Lying flat on her bed as I should have expected, she stretched out her hand to me without a word or a smile, then gave me a packet, which I opened.

"You don't have a cigarette-holder," she said. "The tortoiseshell on this one is as soft to the touch as a woman's cheek."

I opened my mouth to thank her, astonished and confused to have a present like the others for the first time, and such a pretty present. (It was the first year I'd seen Laurette in Paris for Christmas.) She did not give me time to say a word.

"Why did you desert me? . . ." she began, a frown on her forehead and a glint in her eye. "You were too cowardly to stay around for the consequences of your blunder."

Oh, what constancy in Laurette to pick up her reproaches exactly where she left them after almost two weeks of silence and absence! What's more, she asked me nothing whatever about my disappearance. I, on the other hand, had come to her refreshed, full of beneficent fluids, and she taxed me with her bad temper and exasperating monotony as though I were a worthless drudge . . .

In silence I let her harp on. I was cold and patient. At last, she shut up. The evil glint in her eye was extinguished. She murmured, "I think I would give my life to see Aimée back here for five minutes, come of her own accord, even if I were never to see her again . . ."

I was quite moved by this speech and resisted shrugging my shoulders. But I could not stop myself saying, "That would give you four minutes of happiness, but, at the fifth, you would realize that you do not really care for Madame de Lagres."

Very softly she replied, "True . . ."

Resigned, half-yawning, I asked, "Nothing new?"

"Yes indeed, Marion! Aimée is getting ready to leave the

Talliard woman. They've been having terrible scenes for the last week."

She considered my astonishment with a glacial look, as though it were a breach of good manners.

"Really, Laurette, I just don't get it! Why are you still miserable? You've achieved your goal. You wanted to take Aimée away from the Countess . . ."

She interrupted me.

"I'm not taking her away. She's going of her own accord, it's not the same thing."

"Clearly. That's not in the rules of the game. You were meant to win, and that's that."

I regained all my sangfroid and smiled at the irony.

"She's leaving Talliard to go back to her husband," Laurette snarled, "and I see the woman who's acting as intermediary to fix their broken marriage on a daily basis. The husband is taking a lot of coaxing, but he'll give in because he is still in love with Aimée. Only his family were already trying to remarry him, and that's the cause of all the problems. Aimée is so conventional that she positively cannot bear to live on the fringes of society. She wants to be a proper lady again."

I swallowed down my laugh with a sudden start.

"But that's magnificent, Laurette! You're more than avenged now. This time it's Talliard who is suffering, it's she who is struggling to retrieve her property!"

"Talliard doesn't interest me. That Aimée should return to her husband is more hideous than anything!"

"You'll end up regretting Talliard!"

Calmly scandalous, Laurette replied, "At least she was a woman . . ."

"Why don't you join forces with her against the husband, Laurette?"

Laurette laughed. But it didn't last. Still out of breath from this gay outburst, she looked agonized.

"It's a shame . . ."

"What's a shame, Laurette?"

"Everything . . ."

We fell silent, as though some great mystery were at hand. So I put my cigarettes away in the tortoiseshell case with its gold rim, lit one, and said, bravely, somberly, for I envied her return to the straight and narrow, "Aimée is right!"

Laurette didn't pounce. Her left eyebrow rose slowly.

"Too bad for her."

Whereupon I nearly lost my temper with her.

"Listen, Laurette! That's enough now! You must stop being sad. It's a fad you've taken up. Your toy is broken, play another game!"

"I don't feel like playing anything anymore."

I seethed. I raged. I regretted having got caught up in this ridiculous mess. A wave of bourgeois propriety filled me with nausea. I wanted to yell "scandal" and "madman." A priest's indictment of this calmly displayed indecency, this idle sorrow over misfortunes as improper as they were fabricated, shook my whole mutinous being. I hated Laurette, I hated the flesh and its senseless dissipations.

My hands twisted with pain. What was I to reproach others for their sexual fantasies, I who had no sex? A poor impotent figure thrown into the turmoil of women and men, I was not permitted to judge their actions. All I could do was be jealous of their passions, I who could have none; admire from a distance the earthy forces concentrated in their fragile bodies, governing their small souls with the fatal onrush of the tides which rise and fall magnificently in their hour without anything being able to stop them. I was not of the earth, and I was not of heaven, being without faith. I was a figure accursed, and I wanted to curse others?

"Goodbye, Laurette," I said, unable to hide the storm which ravaged me.

She kept my hand in hers and gazed at me for several minutes. Like a strange response to my thoughts, she said, closing her eyes, "You are the only pure and beautiful being I know . . . Everyone else, myself included, is so petty compared with you, so miserable, so useless . . ."

And, turning away to hide her tears, perhaps, she said, "Forgive me . . . Forgive me . . ."

[X]

Alternately irritated and indulgent, distracting Laurette became a kind of passionate duty to Miss Hervin. She came to see her two or three times a week, often stayed for dinner, went out with her, recited poetry for her. From time to time, to conquer this dogged depression, and to win the wager she had made with herself that she would cure Miss Wells—an illusory aim which drew her out of her loneliness—she was tempted to tell her the true story of her life. "But," she thought bitterly, "even that would be of less interest to her than her own obsession. And what terrible consequences for me!"

A month passed, during which Marion occasionally plunged into absence. Upon her return from these week-long disap-

pearances, she found Laurette apathetic, shut up inside her
pain, coming to life only to quarrel, wrangle, ramble, and
harp on about different schemes, one more hare-brained
than the next.

Madame de Lagres's remarriage had its ups and downs,
but her break-up with Countess Talliard was now definitive.
Aimée de Lagres had retreated to a small somber hotel,
awaiting her ex-husband's decision like a chaste and quivering fiancée.

"What an idiot!" Laurette raged.

Forgetting her recent anger, she added, "Poor Talliard has
left for Italy in despair."

Arriving for an update after three days spent far from
Neuilly, Marion sat down one morning on the edge of the
ermine blanket.

"No change? . . . Well, look here, Laurette, are you in-
tending to spend the rest of your existence regretting Aimée?
It's almost like taking the veil, my dear! And what do your
mourners say, Janine, the One-with-the-Red-Hair, Natacha,
and the others?"

"I still see them from time to time, Marion."

"Just enough to make them suffer?"

"Yes."

The chambermaid knocked, came in, and held out a card.

"This lady is downstairs and is asking to see Mademoiselle
immediately."

Laurette did not raise an eyebrow. A little smile played
over her lips as she passed the card, slowly and silently, to
Miss Hervin: "Madame de Lagres."

"Oh! My goodness!" said Marion in a low voice.

"Show her up!" Laurette exclaimed.

Marion had jumped to her feet and was stalking round the room gesticulating wildly.

"I'm off!"

"No, Marion!" Laurette ordered calmly. "On the contrary, you should stay. You'll witness my four minutes of happiness—and the fifth, which will be less so," she added melancholically. "I do believe you've won!"

Her triumph was only discernible from the flicker of flame in her blue eyes; she made no move to sit up, however.

"Oh! Laurette! Laurette!..." Marion began. "Who would have thought..."

She broke off. Aimée de Lagres came in.

She caught sight of Miss Hervin from the doorway and was plainly stopped short in her tracks. For a second she hesitated. Then the impulse was stronger than she was.

"Laurette!..." she cried out.

She had thrown herself on her knees by the bed and kissed Miss Wells's hands as she sobbed. Laurette, her left eyebrow raised, stroked the neck which lay bent over on her sheets.

"I knew you would come back...," she said in her voice from within.

She lifted herself up on one elbow. Her tone was almost maternal.

"Now, now!... you mustn't cry like that!"

Aimée raised her head. Her eyes, full of anguish, and streaming with tears, turned toward Marion, who was still on her feet. And suddenly she accepted her presence at this touching reconciliation. Hand outstretched, eyes cast down, she cried, "Oh! Miss Hervin! You did say that she loved me!"

"Didn't you know that?" Laurette asked softly.

And at that very moment, Marion saw an ironic shadow pass over her face. The four minutes were over. The fifth was beginning.

"Since she is here," Madame de Lagres gulped, "Miss Hervin shall hear everything. I trust her!"

She tore off her hat, hurled it onto the carpet and searched frenziedly for her handkerchief to wipe her nose and eyes. And, still on her knees, she cried, "Laurette, Laurette, you're the only one who can save me! . . . If you only knew!"

"What's the matter then?"

Laurette had just flushed to her hairline. She sat up smartly on her pillows. The expression on her face was already guessing at some melodramatic piece of theater. Aimée was only coming back to her to ask for help and succor. This was no triumph. Her four minutes of happiness were an illusion!

Marion, sitting apart from the others, her chin thrust forward, was knitting her brows.

"Well, I won't beat about the bush!" the young woman declaimed excitedly.

She made a sweeping gesture as of a woman shipwrecked.

"Laurette! Laurette! . . . I'm four and a half months pregnant!"

"Pregnant?" exclaimed Miss Wells and Miss Hervin together.

For a second they exchanged looks over Aimée's head, which was once again buried in the ermine.

"Laurette! Laurette! . . . I've done everything to get rid of it! . . . There's no way! So, do you understand? It's impossible for me to go back to my husband!"

Sitting up again, her hands twisting and turning, she wept so loud she cried out, "There is nothing left for me but to kill myself! . . . Help me! Think of something! Both of you, think of something!"

She fell back down again, her anguished shoulders shook the bed. A short, dreadful silence fell.

"You poor little thing!" Laurette murmured at last.

And all her contempt passed away in this wave of pity.

Imperturbable, she tapped the arms which had been thrown across her.

"Now then! Sit down and tell us what happened."

She added loftily, "You did well to come and see me."

"I did, didn't I?" the young woman stuttered through her tears, adding, as she sat at the edge of the bed, "I knew you were a brick."

"Well? . . ." Laurette asked with a smile.

Marion came and sat down on the other side of the bed. Aimée gazed at them both, her chest heaving, her hanky to her mouth.

"I was so bored with Madame Talliard! So . . . so . . . I took a lover . . . It wasn't easy . . . She kept such a close watch on me . . . I only saw him three or four times . . . And then . . . And then he left . . . He was just a young boy . . . Not rich . . . He left to do his military service . . . in Germany . . . I was not fond enough of him to really miss him . . . But Madame Talliard could see that something was up. Then the rows began. And then I wanted to go back and live with my husband. Oh! how I want to go back and live with my husband! . . . Well, everything began to work out very well . . . And . . . then . . . I noticed it . . . Weeks! . . . Weeks! . . . I've been struggling! . . . All alone . . . Oh! it was awful! . . .

The midwives . . . the . . . All alone! No one in the whole world knows, except you two, now!"

She plunged her fingers into her short hair.

"I am dishonored! Dishonored! What will become of me? . . . And not a penny to my name! I've thrown my whole dowry out the window! If my husband won't take me back, what then?"

Her eyes were no longer looking at the two people listening to her. She gazed upon them emptily, seeing only fate before her.

"I'm sick and tired of being involved in your seedy affairs! I want to go back to my life from before. I want my husband, I want my position!"

At this direct attack, Laurette shook her head, her back straight as on great occasions.

"Our seedy affairs have never given you a child!" she said calmly.

Aimée felt the danger passing. She started kissing Laurette's hands once again.

"You see? You're the one I come to! You're the one I've chosen, because there is only you! Oh! Laurette! . . . Save me!"

"What can we do?" Laurette asked, looking at Miss Hervin.

And suddenly she had the air of a businessman in the middle of a deal.

What impossible scheme would she invent to help out her supplicant? Marion did not want to leave her time to digress.

"Listen!" she said.

She lowered her head to think for a moment. Then she said, "You must answer me perfectly honestly, Aimée."

Aimée felt, at the same time as Laurette, a reassuring authority assert itself in Miss Hervin's tone. They both turned toward her in petrified attention.

"Has your husband decided to take you back?"

"I think he would like to. But he lets his family tell him what to do, and all sorts of other people who want him to make a profitable remarriage and who would be only too happy to discover what has happened to me."

"Fine. Do you think he still loves you?"

"Oh, I'm sure of that!"

"Good. If he still loves you, we've won."

A quiver ran through little de Lagres's body. Her reddened eyes filled magnificently with hope.

"Here's what you have to do . . . ," Marion went on, constructing her scenario as she went along. "Have you written to him yet?"

"Yes."

"Good. You're going to write to him again. You're going to say that you understand his hesitation, that you do not deserve his forgiveness, that you only want him to be happy, that you accept your own misery as long as he is happy. And (believe you me!) you're going to disappear. For a year he must not know where you are hiding nor what has become of you. From time to time you will send him a note of repentance and abnegation; this note will be conveyed by intermediaries, myself for example, who will keep him in ignorance as to your address. Meanwhile, the baby will be born and given to a wet-nurse in the region where you gave birth. And only when you are entirely recovered will you begin to bend a little in your letters and end up suggesting the idea, the hope of a meeting. The first time you finally let him have your address, your husband will reply by begging you to come back, unless he rushes down like a madman to get you himself."

As Marion spoke, Aimée clasped her hands together.

"Oh!" she cried. "Do you really think so?"

"But what if he remarries during that time?" Laurette murmured.

"He won't marry again. He'll be far too busy trying to find out where Aimée is hiding. Even if there weren't a child to conceal, this would be the only tactic to get him back."

"But, on the contrary, won't it make him guess about the child?"

"Look, Laurette! Have a little psychology! How is he going to guess there's a child, given the kind of affairs his wife left him for?"

Whereupon the humorous side of the whole drama struck Laurette's imagination and she began to laugh her finest laugh, rusty, weak, and helpless; her laugh as gay as innocence.

Marion shrugged.

"Instead of laughing, help me decide on the details. We must set to work immediately to find a place in some corner of the provinces where the baby will be born."

"I don't have any money . . ." Madame de Lagres admitted in a whisper.

And her head hung down low.

Laurette took her hand.

"Don't you worry about that, darling . . ."

The embers of laughter which were still playing over Laurette's face now disappeared.

"Marion," she said. "It's up to you to direct us."

Marion was surprised by the palpitation which struck her when these words were spoken. She was being given responsibility for the dangerous adventure they were to face, she was being entrusted with a woman's destiny. Was it anguish she felt? Was it a kind of pleasure, the pleasure of being useful, of living by proxy the events of someone else's life?

"Fine," she said. "But I still have a lot of questions to ask in order to understand the situation fully."

"You'll both stay to lunch with me," Laurette decided. "I'm not going out till this evening. We'll have the afternoon to make plans."

There followed a moment's silence, each one of them absorbed in the gravity of the present and the future. Then Laurette, her mouth turned up at the corners, hissed in conclusion, "A baby! You tricked us all right royally, Aimée, without mentioning your husband."

With a return of gaiety she added, "Perhaps in the end he would have been happy to see you come home pregnant. It would reassure him about your behavior while you were away from him . . ."

Intermezzo

The ambiguous silhouette of a figure with two faces can be seen prowling, but never participating, at various carnivals in modern dress: Julien Midalge's studio, Laurette Wells's villa, Ginette Lobre's bear pit, one or two opium dens, certain cabarets, certain negro balls.

The real bourgeoisie does not frequent these places, or rather what is left of the real bourgeoisie in a Paris heading more and more toward a confusion of the genders, a Paris in which the society of the post-war years[1] is toppling the divisive barriers one after another, leaving only an undifferentiated, multicolored mob, whose numbers are increased by the surreptitious invasion of the foreigner, adding an extra intensity to the colors of this phrenetic Harlequinade.

Alone of his kind amidst an onslaught of lust, ambition, vanity, and stupidity, the unique audience for whom the immense drama is played out, his laugh becomes more and more pronounced each day. Life has no meaning for Marion in this role of neuter surrounded by the battle of desires. Bitter pastime! Too long an exile among human beings for a despairing archangel who does not believe in heaven.

Where should he go?

Why, he should stay here!

What should he do?

Why, work to make a living!

"Bobo, the story of everything!"

"What a fine play I made them perform without ever writing it down!"

Now that Aimée had given birth, the child been placed with a wet-nurse, the husband remarried to his wife, a martyr to remorse and abnegation; now that Laurette had recovered and taken up the normal course of her abnormal life, why would the villa in Neuilly continue to witness the comings and goings of a Miss Hervin, excited by her struggle to save the unhappy woman in whom she was only slightly interested?

Stay here and work to make a living, until death, the great leveler, makes the "unfortunate individual," excluded from life, into so much dust to resemble that of all the others, the only hope permitted his humble and raging desire to be like everyone else.

Je ferai mon squelette aussi bien que les autres[2]

An alexandrine discovered one sleepless night in Marie Noël's admirable book will henceforth be the consoling lullaby of a life which, from the day of his birth, has been so monstrously desolate.

[XI]

With four in the car and Charlie up front next to the driver, and the car roof down so she could add her twopenceworth to the conversation, how would any of them have had time to watch the countryside fly by?

Charlie, the new presence in Laurette's life, spoke English with some unidentifiable American accent, to the irritated amusement of Lord Hampton, who refused to understand a single syllable of her formidably nasal slang.

Though somewhat chubby, Charlie was nonetheless dressed like a man, except for a short skirt, under which she felt it necessary to wear leggings as though she were going off to war.

"Let me drive!" she had said as they set off. "I'll take you to Solesmes at a hundred kilometers an hour, since that's where you've decided to go."

But neither the driver nor Laurette had agreed. Charlie had shown herself to be too reckless in every way, recklessness being a fundamental part of her nature, people said, a fact which was borne out, moreover, by her dress, her almost-shaven head, her remarks, her insolence, the cigars she smoked, everything, in fact, down to her smallest gesture.

Amid all this artless mannishness, two fat pearls shone paradoxically at her ears.

Despite the sharpness in the air, that Palm Sunday the cherry and pear trees of April swayed like vast baskets full of birds along the road. A little round snow-laden cloud floated in the blue above, as though one of those white trees had suddenly taken off into the sky.

The pleasant mildness of the Sarthes was beginning.

"Laurette, why are we going to Solesmes, or wherever it is?" Charlie asked, turning right round on her seat.

"Because Marion and Cecil said there were men there from the Middle Ages and we should go to Mass tomorrow."

"Do you really mean to say we have to go to Mass?" Charlie roared with laughter.

And the woman sitting on the back seat between Marion and Laurette, Iffet Effendi, a Turkish princess, raised her beautiful dark eyes to heaven with the weary look of an exotic beast. She rolled her Rs, warbling like all the women of her country, and replied in perfect English.

"Even I who am Muslim, know more than you! Solesmes is a famous abbey."

"Solesmes! The Benedictine monks!!" Lord Hampton cried scornfully, endangering the stability of his perch at the ladies' feet. "Have you never heard of it?"

"Solesmes and the Easter Mass," Marion continued more softly, "which dates back to Charles the Fifth!"

"Are you sure?" Lord Hampton asked with interest.

"Marion knows everything!" pronounced Laurette.

Charlie was whistling a snatch of ragtime into the wind.

While she pursued the learned conversation she had just started with Lord Hampton, Miss Hervin did not take her eyes off the sights of spring. How long had it been since she last saw the countryside? Her mind saturated with Paris, with its stone, its iron, its trees confined in asphalt, she marveled silently at everything they passed to the left and right of the car. Oh to stop the car! To get out! To breathe it all in! To touch! . . .

And sure enough, as they drove into a narrow road, in the middle of the country, with no sign posts, untarred and completely deserted, a tire burst, the car skidded, the passengers shouted in alarm, and they stopped next to a ditch full of grass, under trees whose buds had only just opened.

"We should take advantage of the stop and have tea!" Charlie pronounced. "It's tea time!"

And when everyone had got out, the little band of travelers settled themselves on the grass next to the road.

"Here are the cakes, here's the thermos, here are the cups!" Charlie went on, very proud of her reputation as a good manager.

"I never drink tea," Laurette declared. "I must have a glass of water. I'm dying of thirst. Maybe there's a stream near here?"

"Stay there," Charlie said, full of importance. "I'll go and find you some. There's a farm just round the bend."

"I'll go with you!" cried Marion, eager to walk in the greenery.

"Me too!" said the Turk.

Sitting down next to Laurette, Lord Hampton said, "We'll wait for you!"

They set off toward the farm. A man appeared on the path, driving two peaceful cows before him.

"They're not on a leash!" exclaimed Charlie, stopping still in her tracks.

And the Turk, astonished, bent toward Marion and murmured in French, "She's scared!"

"Her?"

"I assure you, my dear!"

"That's rich!"

Taking the lead to go past them, Marion moved forward, followed by the Turk with Charlie clutching their arms. One of the cows moved aside, her head held low, away from these strange women who had startled her. Charlie's piercing cry was followed by a fleeing leap. Grabbing the trunk of a tree, with a comic gesture, she made as if to climb it. Marion's laughter was stifled in her throat as always; the Hanoum Effendi's rang out loud and clear.

"Really! What's the point of dressing like a boy?"

Charlie walked back to them, looking pale.

"I was just trying to make you laugh. It worked, didn't it?"

But she didn't dare insist on this lie.

As they returned with their bottle of water, the Turk turned cruel.

"Charlie saved us from the horns of a bull!" she re-counted.

"A bull, those two poor cows we saw going past?" Lord Hampton said in amazement.

And Marion continued in French, which was unintelligible to Charlie, "Laurette, your matamore is just a big ninny!"

Between mouthfuls of water, Laurette replied impassively, "That's always the way when they dress like men. You can tell in advance that they're sissies—and I mean in every regard!"

"What are you talking about?" Charlie asked uneasily.

But Laurette did not deign to reply. In a hurry as always, though there was no reason for it whatever, she wanted to set off immediately. The spare wheel was put on. They drove off again in the intangible spring air.

Marion stifled her sighs.

Their arrival at the only hotel one can stay at while visiting the abbey must have left an unforgettable memory, even though almost all the literary lights of Paris have passed through its doors.

Cold, imperious, and speaking in a murmur, Laurette gave disgruntled orders as soon as she walked in the door. Her bad temper, Marion's appearance, Charlie's appearance, which was even more striking, the Princess with her eyes like a houri,[1] thick with mascara, Cecil Hampton's air of irritated nonchalance, this extraordinary band who asked for bath-rooms when even bathtubs were unknown in the area, who demanded quiet rooms and wanted to order an elegant din-ner, caused a revolution in the poor inn.

"It's cold!" Laurette complained as soon as she was shown her room. "Why are there no carpets on those ghastly tiles?"

In the room next to hers, Charlie was lighting a cigar. Further down, the Turk was freshening up her rouge in front of the cloudy looking-glass. Only Lord Hampton and Marion, lost in the endless corridors, went on talking about Solesmes while they smoked.

"What time is Mass tomorrow?" Miss Hervin asked the frantic boy who went past them carrying two little jugs of hot water.

"Nine o'clock."

"We'll be the only ones going, you'll see!" Lord Hampton predicted.

And he was proved right.

"Oh! . . . why are you waking me up so early, Marion?" Laurette grumbled the next morning.

"Oh, come on! We came here for the Easter Mass!"

"Let me sleep. Charlie's not going, nor is Iffet. And this hotel is horrible! We should have spent the night at Le Mans!"

"We followed your program, Laurette!"

"And not one of you knew where we would end up?"

"Go back to sleep, Laurette, go back to sleep! I'm going to finish getting dressed. Bye now! You can start your complaints again at luncheon!"

It was eleven-thirty before she came back and sat on the edge of the bed where Laurette had decided to remain for the midday meal because of the cold.

Miss Wells saw so many dreams and such enchantment in

these eyes returning from Easter Mass that she had the supreme tact to bite back the rush of recriminations waiting on the tip of her tongue.

"Oh! Laurette! . . . It's such a pity you didn't get up! . . . If only you knew!"

"Tell me about it, Marion! It will be much more beautiful than if I had gone!"

Solesmes, the Easter Mass in the basilisk, that long white corridor where the sun streams in through faded stained glass windows; the walls without pictures, without statues; the altar without a tabernacle; the two stone throngs to the right and left of the choir, those figures, sculpted in the fourteenth and fifteenth centuries, seem to have begotten the immaculate procession of living monks; the singing, dating back to the first centuries, issuing from the throats of men forbidden to use the full brilliance of their voices, just as it is forbidden for the sacerdotal robes to display the full brilliance of their colors; the white bishop with his mitre of pale gold around whom have evolved the monks of snow; the snow of the walls illuminating these white monks bordered with sunlight, a nuanced gleam, transparent shadows; this Easter fairyland resembling some still-unknown creed, Marion recounted it all in her deep voice made hoarse with emotion.

"And, Laurette, when the Mass was over, Lord Hampton was bold enough to ask some questions of a monk passing by. He replied so courteously! He saw that we understood their lily-like purity;[2] he explained everything to us, accompanied us to the sacristy, had whole drawers full of gowns spread out before us woven in restrained hues, had the last crozier to be carved in the monastery brought to him, all in ivory with a kneeling angel among the adornments, whose long wings hung down like the elytra[3] of a white insect. What disdain they had for the brash colors of the main Church! The Benedictines are veritable religious aesthetes, the aristocracy of Catholicism. The arts, literature, history, music, they cultivate them all, as well as their beautiful gardens. They love the modern as much as the antique. Their altar has just been completed by a contemporary designer. They have electricity in the basilisk. But that does not prevent them from being emaciated due to severe diet and constant prayer. In the final procession there was a young monk who was so pale, so uplifted . . . Fifteen or sixteen years old maybe . . ."

"He could not have been more uplifted than you, Marion! Are you sure that you were not that young monk?"

Miss Hervin gave a start. At that moment her *abbé*'s exclamation suddenly rose up again in her memory, "He'll become a Benedictine!"

"You've gone silent, Marion?"

"I have no more to say, Laurette."

"Pity! It was so beautiful! I am very glad I came to Solesmes . . ."

The look in her eye changed the topic of conversation even before her words.

"But . . . You haven't forgotten that the original idea was to go and surprise Aimée's child's foster mother?"

"Oh! That's right!" Marion's voice became sober, snatched from its dream.

"Here they are with my luncheon," Miss Wells went on. "Hurry up and eat with the others. We must be back in Paris before nightfall."

Charlie, Iffet, and Lord Hampton, grouped around the car on the road, where they had been told to wait, set their wits to improvising a cocktail from elements provided by Charlie. They hadn't even listened to what Laurette had told them through half-open lips: "Marion and I are going to see the baby of one of my old maids . . ."

What a lot of trouble it took to find the little house forgotten among the cultivated fields where Madame de Lagres's son, "of unknown parentage," was hidden.

It had been two and a half years since the Widow Lagnel, paid regularly by Miss Wells, whose name she didn't know, had seen the two ladies in the car who had given her the child.

"The nurse has named him Pierre Petit[4] on his birth certificate. You'll receive the sum agreed upon each month. We were told at the town hall that we could count on your honesty!"

It was by chance that they had chosen the Sarthe region on the map of France. Born in a hole in the Pyrenees, the child was to disappear into the depths of some other part of the country.

Miss Wells's decision to go and surprise this foster mother did not imply any special interest in the innocent victim of Aimée de Lagres's affairs, but rather a little attack of avarice as befell her from time to time. For a while the Widow Lagnel had been sending letter after letter to Miss Wells's lawyer's address, the only one she had been given, asking for an increase in the allowance paid, since the cost of living had gone up again.

Angry about the time they had wasted looking for the little house, as well as about everything else, Laurette had already assumed her steely eye and straight back as she crossed the little garden. Marion followed her absently, smoking a cigarette, entirely absorbed in her Benedictine dreams.

A little gang of children ran up as they approached, the oldest being about ten, the five others decreasing in age down to the smallest infant.

Curiosity spurred them to go and meet the fine ladies, but as soon as they came near, Marion's cigarette froze them to the spot.

"Are you the Lagnel children?" Laurette asked in frozen tones.

"Yes M'Lady . . ."

Laurette opened her mouth to ask "Which one is the foster-child?" but she stopped short. It was not hard to recognize him in the shabby garments of a poor child. Sickly and fearful, already at two and half he was clearly of a different race than the rest of the gang with their ruddy cheeks and peasant build. He had Aimée's melancholy eye-lids and her aristocratic hands. The rest of his small person must have taken after his father. His blond baby hair fell in dusty curls over his golden brown eyes. Snotty-nosed and shy, he hid behind one of the girls.

Widow Lagnel hurried to meet them. She recognized the fine ladies and, visibly put out, launched into excuses for the children's untidy appearance, with a quantity of explanations about the difficulty of keeping them clean, much groaning over the harshness of the times and the bad luck of becoming a widow with five children to raise.

"The sixth pays for the others!" Laurette scornfully cut her short.

She had generously agreed to Aimée's salvation and its financial consequences, but she intended to have her fill of accusations and criticism, since that was what she had come for.

"With five kids and that one into the bargain!" the peasant woman repeated stubbornly.

"You shouldn't have had so many!"

"And we are so poor!" continued the other, who hadn't heard.

"I loathe the poor!" said Laurette.

But her voice was so low that this too was lost.

"Will the ladies come into the house . . ."

Widow Lagnel was all pleasant attention.

They went in. Leaving the others outside, the foster mother had taken her charge up in her arms. He yelled and kicked.

"Now, now, little Pierre! Now, now!"

"Put him out!" Laurette ordered. "We can't hear ourselves think and I need to talk to you."

The oldest of the urchins was called and led young Pierre Petit away. They did not see him again. The bitter discussion began.

The sun was going down when Marion and Laurette reappeared. The other three were merry from the cocktails and greeted them with shouts and laughter. But Laurette got more and more irritable and their gaiety gradually turned to peevishness on the long ride home. By the time they reached Paris, Charlie and the Turk were not speaking to each other, and Laurette had once again fallen out with Lord Hampton.

[XII]

In order to give herself up entirely to her new preoccupation—Solesmes—Marion felt the need to be a man. A very different kind of solitude from that of Passy awaited him at his already monkish apartment on the left bank.

It was the first time his writing table had seen the poet engaged in anything other than work on other people's writing or the composition of poetry. By some mysterious compulsion he needed to be seated in the same place where his mind had toiled over literary labor. Only there was he at ease to think.

The mystical figure of the young monk at Easter . . . Obsession! To be that himself, to serve Mass, to dress in the same archangelical whiteness in that otherworldly atmosphere; to wear masculine robes until the day he died, the only garments possible for him; no longer to maintain any contact with ordinary existence, had not the voices of his childhood prophesied his destiny, the only one suitable for him?

"He'll become a Benedictine!"

Before these words had represented only an empty formula. Since his visit to Solesmes, they were written in miraculous letters made of light, on the walls, on the ground, in the sky, even in the darkness, everywhere his unseeing eyes turned.

"What is there to prevent me becoming a monk? . . . I am used to working anonymously, I'm used to silence, I'm used to concentrating. I could fast for as long as anyone wanted. I am sexless. I am weary of life . . ."

He put his head in his hands as he tried to believe. That was all he lacked: faith.

The catechism? A piece of childhood drudgery. Bitterly he reviewed his *abbés,* one after the other, then the Jesuits at the college. No outstanding priest had appeared in his life. Those he had known were no more than colorless memories. He had gradually constructed his own mystical realm by himself, or rather the religious fairy tale which he often murmured to himself. The cathedrals in which he had dreamed, the music of Bach, for him, this was what God was. It was at this he had sometimes cried out, "I believe!" But he knew quite well it was not enough. The torch which burned in him, the flame rising up toward the heights, fell back at each gust of wind with the acrid fumes of despair.

When one says "I believe," one must say it continually, and not only at moments of lyricism. One must say it during the lean times that life doles out to all, even to monks. One must say it from the depths of the daily grind, say it when one is in pain, when one is miserable, insignificant, say it when time hangs on one's hands, when the heart beats at its normal pace. One must say it as though one were saying "I know," without weakening, without doubting, without tiring, without getting impatient at the slow pace of life before the hour of death, the blessed hour when one ceases to be that paltry thing: a human being . . .

No vague aspiration quickly forgotten at the slightest frivolous excuse. To be not only a believer, but a Catholic, to *choose* one's native religion, to be Catholic as one is French, as one bears the name of one's father . . .

"First I must go and find a priest," he told himself courageously. "Begin at the beginning . . ."

But he had seen more than enough priests. What if he fell upon a Philistine with the difficult secret he had first to confide!

Books! Why not try to instruct himself in the silence and perfection of the written word?

He turned in his chair to look in the appropriate direction. He knew where to find the first book of the night among the leather-bound spines which, like the pipes of a great organ, surrounded his humble bedroom.

Slowly he got up.

He did not have to search for long before he put his hand on a small black book: the Gospels.

And, under his studious little lamp, he began the warrior's vigil.[1]

I knew it . . . So many contradictions . . . And it's so far from Catholicism! The Western graft has made the uncomplicated

Eastern tree bring forth lofty, extravagant flowers: the cathedrals, the beauties of worship, Rome and its pure white Pope
who, seated on his throne with his tiara on his head, seems a
direct descendant of Heliogabalus. Is there even an allusion
to this in the words of Jesus?

The Protestants would seem closer to it than we are. But
then, how dry, and what erring forays into "freethinking"!

But I should not get discouraged so quickly. There are
replies to my objections. I dread hearing them on the banal
lips of any mediocre priest. First I shall study the liturgy,
which I scarcely know. There is color, there is poetry. Without tangible beauty and without arcane wisdom, Protestantism has nothing to attract me. I prefer absurdity decked out
in gold, enveloped in incense.

Only incense, and all its perfumes contain, might one day
allow me to become a Catholic.

But there is also the study of theology, and here we fall into
complications and extravagance. I am out of my depth. I try
to cling on. Catholicism has been my tradition for centuries,
it is one of the colors of my coat of arms. I love it atavistically
before loving it personally. A priest! A priest who knows
how to listen to me, and then respond!

Each Sunday I go to Mass in my parish church. All is
beautiful from the beauty of long centuries which live on in
the Sunday ceremony; all is beautiful until the moment the
sermon begins! Ouch! We fall back into the secular, the
human, and so into mediocrity. Between the two, it is an
unequal balance.

Miserable dreamer, it is through humanity and its dreary
horror that one must become and remain a believer. But

when one has the misfortune of being a poet, how hard it is to approach the sublime by so many small paths devoid of charm!

To take charm into consideration is, once again, to make a toy of the things of the earth. The things of the earth should be no more than what they call *the trial,* a long penitence in the shadows before the joy of the ultimate light.

I would like to write to the monk who greeted us so warmly at Solesmes. But I don't know his name. I could go back to Solesmes in my masculine garb, and alone. But how do I approach this monk? And how do I know he is the soul I need?

I am frightened. And even if he was the soul I need, how would I ever dare tell him who I am? Would they ever accept me in a men's monastery with the feminine element contained within me? Neither a Benedictine monk, nor a Benedictine nun. Both doors will close before me—as always.

It is better not to go back there. I shall rock my dreams of monkhood for a long time like a fine secret to console myself. I don't want to spoil that. In my dream monastery I can be happy in silence.

Perhaps fate will allow me suddenly to meet the priest I need. At Mass I pray as I may. And then I watch the surplices go by, and I think, "Could this be the one? Could this be the one?"

I was already more than chaste, being neuter. My horror of the flesh became more pronounced as the weeks of research went past.

Nevertheless, I was obliged to work if I didn't want to starve to death, obliged to interrupt my reading and meditation to get back to a page in a novel, an act of a play; I was obliged to go to Ginette's, and in that writing, in those eyes which met my own, there was only one thing: the flesh! What nauseating meat-trade! I would have liked to see no one, I would have liked to close myself up in my burning desire to believe, my frenzied studies to make myself believe. I hardly slept anymore. My lowly tasks were over, I was going back to my books, to ask them for initiation, illumination . . .

To no avail, my God! The more I read the further I was from my goal.

Solesmes! Solesmes!

Last winter Midalge spoke to me of the little Dadaist poetess, Simone Luvedier (often seen at his house) who suddenly converted.

One evening I took it upon myself to go to that dissolute studio. What a stroke of light, I thought! That's who I need, and none other. Why did I not think of it earlier? But Midalge must have lost sight of her by now. She must no longer frequent such places. Never mind! Let's try.

"Why my dear, I shall arrange a rendez-vous!" Midalge told me.

And that's how it was. This morning I went to Simone Luvedier's. I found her as made up as before, wearing extravagant pajamas, surrounded by rare furnishings. She spoke to me about her conversion as though it were a literary matter, making ingenious comparisons in a thousand pretty turns of phrase. Her musical voice said repeatedly, "The Thomists, my dear!"[2] She seemed at ease in the subject, as though in another pair of luxurious pajamas. She is preparing a dazzling book, under the auspices of the clergy. I got the impression she was being pampered by certain elements in the religious world, like an important little star. I left her house in terror. What should I do? What was to become of me?

Sensing that she would need to take to her bed for a long time, her body wracked with exhaustion and fever, Marion hurried to return to her more comfortable apartment in the sixteenth. Miss Hervin would pay dearly for the torments of the little Valdeclare.

"What a condition Mademoiselle is returning in!" Madame Creponnet exclaimed. "The Channel crossing must have been bad this time round!"

"Very bad . . ." said Marion, who was fainting with fatigue.

Miss Hervin begged the concierge to burn in front of her the numerous letters and telegrams from Laurette which lay collecting dust. From the depths of her bed, the figure on the edge of collapse tried to smile at the simple soul who was shaking her head.

"And to think that Mademoiselle won't see a doctor!"

"Nothing in the world could induce me, Madame Creponnet! I know how to cure myself. I need to sleep, sleep. That's all. As soon as I'm able, I'll try to eat to build up my strength. You see, I don't even smoke any more. But I have my little sleeping pills. That's the only thing that'll save me."

"But a lady has been here twice already while Mademoiselle was away. If she comes back . . ."

"You'll tell her I'm still away. I don't want to see anyone. No one at all. Less even than usual . . ."

I must have something like brain fever, but I won't be lucky enough to die of it. Solesmes! Solesmes! I am in Hell. Quick, my pills. I'll take them with the milk Madame Creponnet put there for the night. When I'm back on my feet, if I recover, I must travel. Why not really go to London, where I've never yet set foot? I was very well paid for the last play I took to Ginette. I have some money. London. A good dose of Protestantism . . . Hail Mary . . . My God, if you exist, let me see your light! Did Luvedier's pajama suit look like Midalge's? . . . The little dark-haired man nearly threw himself on his knees when I walked into Midalge's that evening. But Laurette's letters have been burnt and her visits rejected in advance . . . Luvedier's pajama suit and the young monk's white robe . . . I would not like to be a Benedictine nun . . . I thought I was a boy until I was fifteen years old! Solesmes! Solesmes! Solesmes! He will become a Benedictine . . . dictine, dictine, dictine . . . dict . . . Thank you, nothingness!

[XIII]

The next time Miss Hervin saw Laurette, she was dressed all in white, on her feet in her large salon. After more than seven months of silence and absence, she greeted Miss Hervin without a smile, holding out an apple she was munching instead, with the scarcely audible words, "Take a bite! It's delicious!"

She brought the apple right up to Marion's mouth, and, half-heartedly, Marion bit into it.

"Your lips are pale. Have you been ill all this time?"

"Yes, a little."

"In London?"

"In London."

"But why did you go to London, and for such a long time?" said Miss Wells, thinking about something else.

Marion did not reply. She knew the interrogation would

go no further. She had made up her mind to come because the last of Laurette's indefatigable notes read, "If you're back, come and have lunch at Neuilly. I need you for a new trip to Sarthe."

"Mademoiselle is served . . . ," announced the valet.

They went through to the dining room. During lunch, served without bread or tablecloth as always, they spoke English. As she attacked the plover's eggs, Laurette told Marion how she had just received some poems by an unknown author, which seemed to her beautiful.

"You will read them to me presently, Marion."

A little strangling sound made Marion's voice sound even odder than usual.

"So you're going back to Sarthe?"

"Yes, tomorrow. Will you come with me?"

"Why not? Are you bringing anyone else?"

"No, Marion. No one but the two of us. It's because of that ghastly nurse. Aimée's child fell down, or something. They plastered him up wrong. It'll take a specialist to set it right, so pots of money. But none of it may be true. I have to go and take a look."

"And," Marion controlled herself, "do you think we will also go to . . ."

"Your abbey? Yes, if it pleases you."

"Why *my* abbey?" Marion shivered.

"Because you told me it was so beautiful. I'll try and go with you this time. But we want nothing more to do with that disgusting hotel. We'll go to Le Mans."

"We'll go to Le Mans . . . ," Marion echoed, no longer aware of what she was saying.

She managed to get a grip of herself and talk of other things.

"You don't want any wine?" asked Miss Wells.

"No. I don't drink it anymore."

When they reached dessert:

"Here are the cigarettes, Marion."

"No thank you! I don't smoke anymore."

"You don't! How extraordinary! Why?"

"Tobacco is a form of slavery. I want to be free."

"And what do you do with so much freedom?"

"Oh! What do I do with it!"

Marion looked away. The end of November darkened the bow-window with its tracery of black branches, its low, fleeting grays[1] and sudden downpour.

"It's cold," said Laurette. "Tomorrow we'll take the saloon car."

They made their journey in endless rain, huddled up against each other under the car rug, a hot-water bottle at their feet. They had left too late. Night fell quickly. The headlamps transformed the gaunt, black countryside into a luminous fairyland. Laurette's poetic imagination found some ravishing comparisons to greet these sights. Immersed in her dream, Marion barely heard her. Her heart was beating like a lover in legend who is going to meet his fiancée and is afraid, afraid of finding her less beautiful than his memory or, on the contrary, more beautiful but ready to say no. For seven months Solesmes had tortured his mind and filled his soul. What would happen after this second visit? Spring was no longer there to wrap everything in wonder, no ceremony was being prepared in the basilisk. No Easter splendor. The monastery in its strict daily routine, nothing more.

"So much the better! . . . It will be closer to the truth!"

It would not be difficult to find the monk again, learn his name. Then letters would be exchanged. Then . . .

"The little drops on the windows are more beautiful than my opals."

"How true, Laurette!"

"Look at the blue grotto we're driving into. We're heading toward the home of the mermaids."

"Yes, the home of the mermaids, Laurette. I can hear them calling from afar . . ."

But it was Le Mans they stopped at, and Miss Wells became irritable and shrewish as soon as she opened the door of the hotel.

"I assure you, Marion, it's better to go to the nurse's house first. Night will not yet have fallen when we reach Solesmes."

There was nothing to do but obey. Bitterly Marion regretted not being master of car, time, and whim. The chauffeur had no trouble finding the little house again. Without the flowering trees in the little garden, it looked sinister at the bottom of the muddy hollow under the ceaseless rain. Annoyed at having to walk across the mud, Laurette began to prepare her icy thunderbolts.

Widow Lagnel came to the door, dumbfounded at the sight of the two of them. The ceaseless activity of the children, a smell of humidity and warm iron from the sheet-metal of the roof, the oozing of the walls, the squalor of this dwelling, which was too small for so many people, the chiaroscuro with which their poverty was permeated, caused

Miss Wells to back away and utter a thoroughly Anglo-Saxon "Ugh!"

The nurse was already talking loudly, anticipating the nasty remarks to come.

"The children are not at school because the two oldest have colds and the other three are too small to go by themselves. It's far from here, see, and night comes on quickly at home time. So, with the weather being what it is and them forced to stay indoors, it's not surprising they've put the house in this state. The ladies know what children are like. I've just washed the floor. That doesn't help any. If I had known you were coming, everything would be better, of course, and little Pierre's bed would be a bit whiter than it is. But there's two of them sleep in it at night, and we're not rich people as can afford to change the sheets every day."

"It's when we're not here that it should be clean!" Laurette interrupted, trying to get a word in. "I see you have no idea of hygiene! You earn enough with the foster child not to live in a stable. Where is he?"

"There . . . ," the woman pointed, sour-faced, ready to defend herself.

"Two in this bed at night, you say?" Laurette repeated. "Two of them in this dirt? And he's ill? What exactly is wrong with him?"

"He never got back his strength since he fell off of the ladder and the doctor from round here plastered him up."

"He's still in plaster?" Laurette asked, looking with distant disgust at the pale little thing lying helpless on the bed.

"No, he ain't no more!" the nurse said aggressively. "But he's none the better for that. As for getting him to put a foot on the ground, don't even think about it. That's why I wrote that the doctor said only a specialist would be able to set him right."

"And that's why we've come!" Laurette replied severely.

The woman crossed her arms, surrounded by her attentive but jiggling brood. One of the little girls touched Miss Wells's fur.

"Can't you send your children away? There are too many for me."

"And where do you want me to send them in this cold? This is the only room that's heated."

Marion, whose dreams were constricted by all this reality, sat down resignedly on the chair she found near the sick child's bed. The others were still standing up.

"Given what Laurette's like, we'll be here for over an hour. We'll never reach Solesmes before nightfall."

Her foot drummed impatiently on the floorboards surrounded by the children's din. The shrill voice of the peasant woman rose above everything.

"You've come here to quarrel with me, I can tell! But I won't let myself be browbeaten by you . . ."

Laurette started up at the same time, "If you're going to be insolent into the bargain, I shall have them prove you are responsible for everything. First of all, how did that little boy fall from a ladder at three years old?"

The two voices blended into each other like the noise of battle. After a quarter of an hour of violent argument, a little girl began to howl.

At that moment Marion started. She had just been thinking, "To love God! To have such a friend—God!"

A little feverish hand placed itself on hers and nearly made her cry out. The contact surprised and disgusted her. As she quickly pulled back her fingers, from the depths of the bed near which she was sitting, she heard the small voice say weakly, "I love you, I do . . ."

She turned her head. Aimée de Lagres's son, immobilized on his filthy pillow, was looking at her with his great golden eyes, a little fearful, but magnetized by the only being in the fray who remained silent, so silent beside his bed.

Sudden pity tore her from her mute prayer. "Born of unknown parentage . . . ," she thought. "Poor little aristocrat thrown into this lice-ridden bed, in the middle of this coarse family, and he doesn't even know he is a victim . . ."

She bent over and stared at the sick child, without thinking of replying to his touching little declaration. She did not understand children, had never looked at any close up.

"Injustice . . . ," she continued. "Monstrous egotism, iniquity!"

The little boy, bothered by her staring eyes, raised his arm to his face so that he should not see her any more.

"Fine, then!" Laurette was summing up in a quiver of rage. "As I drive back through Le Mans I shall go and see the specialist. He will come and examine the child and send his bill to me. You shan't have the money."

"Mama! Mama!" yelled the children.

The cramped walls were filled with the increased racket. Laurette's shoulders shifted higher and higher. The nurse's face became hideous.

How long did the scene go on? Finally:

"Come, Marion! We won't stay here a minute longer! It smells too bad and it's too ugly!"

Widow Lagnel closed the door on them without daring to slam it openly. In the dark little garden, the rain went on falling.

As soon as they were in the car, Laurette exclaimed, "And to think that now Aimée has returned to the straight and narrow, she no longer sees me for fear her husband find out!"

Her short angry laugh despised the whole of humanity.

"That child will die," Miss Wells went on. "Which is the best thing that could happen to him."

"We must take him away from there," said Marion. "It's simply horrible."

"Then where would we put him?" retorted Laurette dryly. "Do you want to take him?"

Marion couldn't stop herself laughing.

The noise of the engine and the sticky sound of the tires on the wet roadway rose above the rather hostile silence.

A little later Miss Hervin asked timidly, "Are we still going to Solesmes?"

"I promised you we would!" Laurette grunted.

Before the third turning, night began to fall with the rain. From moment to moment, Marion's resentment grew worse. Laurette's obstinacy in insisting on first going to see the nurse, when it was only logical to start at the abbey, filled her with an indignation bordering on hatred. "She always makes us miss everything!"

Laurette, as testy as Marion, kept quiet, her silence full of interminable reproaches. The headlamps went on.

"It's not worth going anymore!" Marion exclaimed grimly.

"You could have said so earlier!"

"I told you when we set off. We should have gone to Solesmes first."

"Solesmes was less important than the other business."

Concentrating on remaining distant, they did not look at each other.

"You don't need daylight to pick a quarrel, you need it to visit a church."

"Yes, but visiting a church is an extra one can do without if need be."

"With two-cents-worth of organization, we could very well have done both."

"I first accomplished what I came for. I'm not keen on putting myself out for nothing."

"You would not have put yourself out for nothing, we would have done both things in time."

"I call being in time arriving at exactly the right moment."

"The moment would have been the same an hour and a half later."

"We didn't know that. Widow Lagnel might not have been in."

"How absurd! Where might she have been, then?"

"Do you know what her habits are?"

"I don't need to know her habits. Her house is miles from anywhere and it was pouring with rain."

"Precisely."

"Precisely what?"

"She could have gone shopping."

"Shopping at that time, in the country, and at this season of the year?"

"One does one's shopping when one can, even in the country."

"Don't make me laugh! After all this, we won't be able to see a thing."

"We saw what we needed to see."

"Then tell your chauffeur to go back to Paris."

"This is a fine time, now that you've made us make this useless detour!"

"It would not have been a detour if we had started here."

"But it would have been wrong to start here!"

Marion's hands were shaking. Miss Wells went on. Only silence replied. When the car finally stopped, she said, "Well then, here we are! Are you satisfied?"

The chauffeur opened the door in the black downpour; from her seat in the shadows, Marion caught sight of the wicket gate which led to the monastery. How could she ring at this time, without a name to give? And even if they went to fetch a monk, what should she say to him?

"Well? . . . Aren't you going to get out?" Laurette asked in exasperation.

Marion slammed the door shut again.

"No! Can't you see it would be ridiculous?"

"What's ridiculous is making us drive out here for nothing!"

Marion lowered the window in front.

"To Paris!" she ordered the driver.

And Laurette could surely not imagine what bleak despair those two words contained.

[XIV]

Miss Hervin was awakened with a start next morning by a telegram which had been written out the previous day. She had only just got to sleep after a feverish night.

"Laurette is really too hateful."

Tearing open the envelope with a gesture that could kill, she read, "A. should know all the same. See to it."

After hours of prostration, a furious irony revitalized her. She hurried through her toilette. And laughed with rage.

As soon as she was ready, she sat at her little desk.

Her reply: "See to it yourself. No time."

She was about to get up and run to the post office. But she stayed slumped in her chair, the palm of her hand over her eyes.

Wasn't it better to smoke cigarettes and drink wine than

to let the spirit of vengeance have its way at the first prompting?

Slowly she tore up her piece of paper. With an indescribable effort, all her faculties strove to let mercy into her heart, and even penitence.

It was certainly more beautiful, more productive than a visit to Solesmes.

Charity is not a theme for meditation, but for practical acts. By subtle casuistry, it was necessary to prove the following: that Laurette, with all her vices, her churlish method of doing good, and her perpetual irritation, displayed more altruism than Marion, the future Benedictine. Only the total counted, after the first two additions had been made. On one side: immediate help to the sick child, perfectly disinterested actions toward the ungrateful Aimée; on the other: the pleasure of embracing a dream by accepting the kind offer of a place in a car.

"I didn't see anything, but the intention was there . . ."

Sighing hugely, Marion managed to persuade herself. It was for her to bow low and give thanks for the fine example. And how could she give thanks if not by fulfilling the favor asked of her, a favor that, furthermore, concerned once again the little tot whose life was in danger?

"For he will die . . . ," Miss Hervin pronounced out loud, as she picked up her hat.

She was struck by this lack of real pity for the poor little martyr. Amid the agitation and irritation of the previous day, only one tender word had been spoken, on the lips of a three year old, from the depths of a bed of sickness: "I love you, I do . . ."

Yet no response, no smile recognized this sweetness. What

lack of courtesy! What disappointment, perhaps, for the baby!

"I love you, I do . . ." That was worth the journey; for this was the first time innocent lips had said such a thing to the "unfortunate individual" all alone in the world, surrounded by degenerates. And yet it had taken a line of argument as laborious as a mathematical calculation to allow those five words into her heart.

Tears? Her hat thrust roughly down around her eyes, Miss Hervin hurried out to fulfill the mission entrusted to her by Laurette.

Before taking up watch again as she had during Talliard's days, she had the very simple idea of going first to find out whether Madame de Lagres was in Paris.

During the bus journey toward the Plaine Monceau, she forced herself to dig more deeply into what she had discovered.

"It's no longer a question of acting as go-between in the dubious saga of three idle women, but the life of an unfortunate little human being."

And she was amazed to realize this fact, which had not struck her before. What a serious turn the crazy adventure had taken!

She was gradually filled with the sensation of bending over an abyss which had suddenly opened up in front of her. Then came a terrible question.

Who exactly was responsible for this three-year-old misery, abandoned in the depths of a hovel in Sarthe? Who had decided that to save Aimée de Lagres, an uninteresting little doll, her child should be sacrificed?

At the time all three of you considered it a shameful sickness, a kind of tumor that one gets removed in hiding by an unknown doctor. But now it's born, now it talks, it feels, it will grow up, become a man—if it doesn't die in a couple of months . . . And if it dies in a couple of months? Who then will be the real killer of this life that's just beginning?

Her head held low, Marion went through the carriage entrance of the building where Aimée lived.

"Monsieur and Madame de Lagres? . . . They've been in Egypt for a month . . . When will they be back? We don't know. I think they're going to the East Indies after that."

"Thank you . . . ," Marion said as she closed the door to the concierge's lodge.

And back in the street she began to walk quickly, biting her lips.

Laurette, who was still at lunch, was amazed to see her walk in looking as she did.

"You have not yet eaten, I hope. Sit down. I'll have them bring the dishes back."

"No! I don't want anything to eat! Laurette, something very serious is happening," Marion said in English, emphasizing her words. "First of all, we didn't go back to Le Mans to see that specialist yesterday, and the child is still pinned to his dirty bed. It's my fault more than yours. I nagged you and got on your nerves and you forgot everything else in the quarrel. Just now, when I got your message, I went to find out the whereabouts of the de Lagres. They're both off to the back of beyond for months. So . . . ?"

Marion was so pale Laurette began to watch her closely without replying. Abruptly Laurette stood up.

"Lie down . . . ," she said, catching Marion just in time.

Miss Hervin reopened her eyes in Laurette's arms. She had been laid down on a sofa, in a corner of the bow-window, and the chambermaid was wetting her temples with vinegar while the valet held the bowl.

"How stupid . . . ," she murmured.

Then she closed her eyelids again because the dining room was spinning round and round.

"Come now, Marion, come, come!" Laurette said softly, patting her hands.

Gradually the weakness wore off.

"I beg your pardon . . . I beg your pardon . . ."

"Oh, you gave me such a fright!" Miss Wells sighed, smiling to see her come round.

"Would Mademoiselle like the driver to go and get a doctor?"

"No! No!" replied Marion, trying to get up. "It's nothing—quite over now!"

A moment later, reclining amid a pile of cushions and alone with Laurette, Marion said, "Don't think about that absurd fainting fit a moment longer. You must listen to me, Laurette. We cannot leave that child where he is. It's simply criminal."

"Darling . . . ," Laurette whispered. "You're still so pale. You should look after yourself. You haven't looked well since you got back. You told me you'd been ill? What was it? What was wrong with you?"

"Nothing, I assure you! A little over-exertion. Won't you listen to me?"

"I'll do whatever will make you happy."

"Then let's go back there. We'll take the specialist from Le Mans, or someone else, to the Widow Lagnel's. That little boy needs medical attention as soon as possible. Perhaps the doctor will have a clinic we can put him in?"

Miss Wells tossed her head, stiff-backed all of a sudden.

"Aimée is too much!" she snapped, her eyes hard. "She waltzes off across the world and leaves all the problems to us."

She considered a moment.

"You don't think her child would be better off in a public orphanage?"

"Maybe. Yes, I think he would . . . But first he has to be healed."

"Healed, to do what? Perhaps it was—Providence, is that what you call it?—which made him fall so that he would die?"

"Oh! Laurette!"

At this Marion sat straight up.

"A child is not a little dog or a little cat to be drowned because it's got the mange!"

"Unfortunately," said Laurette with great cruelty.

Marion was on her feet.

"When Aimée gets back I'll do everything I can to speak with her and put her in the picture, get a decision from her, some money . . . But, I repeat, in the meantime . . ."

"You know very well that I will always supply the money since I promised I would," Laurette said, taking offense. "Why are you bringing that up?"

"Forgive me, Laurette, I know what a brick you are. But you don't realize (and I didn't realize either until this morning) that among the three of us, we've done something criminal with that unfortunate child. And I am the guiltiest of all, I who took care of everything as though it were a wretched piece of theater."

"Now, now, Marion, now, now! . . . Don't invent reasons for us to reproach ourselves! We'll go back there, since you're set on it. (We'll end up attracting attention in Sarthe!) Wait a moment! I've thought of something! We'll bring that young man, you know the one, the young scholar you've seen at my house a few times. He's going to be a great surgeon one day, apparently . . . That's it! . . . I've got it now. Let me arrange it. He'll tell us where to put the child to recover, if he can recover. Afterwards, well, we'll see!"

"I never would have thought," she went on with her prettiest laugh, "that I would have to spend so much time on a nurse and a small child. The search for paternity is a fine thing! A most unexpected . . . and most vexing method of playing the man!"

She grew serious again.

"Are you satisfied?"

Hands entwined, "Darling . . . ," she said once more very softly, with a twitch of her left eyebrow.

This new journey presented so many complications that in the end it could not be decided upon until the 20th of December.

"Why not wait until the 24th . . . ," suggested Laurette. "We could go to midnight Mass at Solesmes at the same time. That must be even better than Easter. And anyway it would be fun to spend New Year's Eve somewhere other than Paris."

"Yes, midnight Mass . . . ," Marion mused, closing her eyes.

But with a heroic effort she sacrificed the beautiful mirage.

"No, no! We said the 20th, let's stick to the 20th!"

On the seventeenth she was on foot, walking along a shabby street in the cold, lost in thought.

The little Christmas tree, all alone, with its lighted candles and its tinsel, sitting in the humble shop window, seemed to have the wonders of childhood and the naive imagery of Christmas hanging from its short branches; and with modest eloquence, from the mist of centuries, the penny toys, the stars, the balls, the painted sugar tops which adorned it, amid pictures of hoar frost and sons of the Virgin, it retold the ancient miracle of every year.

Marion stopped short in her tracks and gazed at it. The pain in her heart, which hurt so much at the end of the year, sent her abruptly back into the skin of the little boy of long ago deprived of the universal joy, buried in his ghastly *château* in the Northern beetfields.

"How happy the child who gets that as a present!"

Her hand on her mouth, she skipped a breath.

"Oh! What an idea!"

A few seconds later she went into the shop. In a moment — the time it took to replace the worn-out candles with new ones — she came back out, the awkward bundle in her arms, a little shamefaced, a little joyful, a little melancholy; and her eyes searched hopelessly for the chance taxi which might be passing by there to take her home again.

"What's that?" Laurette demanded in vexation.

They had had to get up early. Naturally she was in a bad temper.

"Why that looks just like a Christmas tree!" said the young intern.

"That's what it is . . . ," Marion acknowledged, her head bowed.

"You're not taking that to the little boy, are you?"

"Yes, Laurette, I am!"

"In the first place, it's going to get in the way in the car. We won't be able to move our feet. And in the second place, it's ridiculous to accustom that child to presents. Leave it here!"

"Oh! Laurette! . . . I beg you!"

With bad grace, Miss Wells let herself be moved. Throughout the whole trip, the little tree, which took up so much space, was to be the heavensent focus of her angry muttering. After an hour, the veins in Marion's temples were ready to burst. Nonetheless, she kept smiling, determined to put a brave face on it. The little doctor was enjoying himself. He had a handsome, serious face and merry eyes. Sitting between the two friends, he was perhaps trying to penetrate the mystery of the outing he was being taken on. Someone had brought him to Miss Wells's house one day and he had often gone back, appreciating, as did all those of refined taste, her unique personality.

Surprise. The house was clean, the children were clean, Widow Lagnel was all smiles.

"Unexpected visits have done you good!" Laurette pro-

nounced immediately, almost disappointed by this atmosphere in which her scolding had no place.

Left behind in the car, the Christmas tree was waiting to
make its royal entrance.

Little Pierre, stretched out as well as he could on two
chairs next to the stove, devoured the invading three-
some with his eyes. The other children came back in
from the garden, but, well-schooled, did not speak or run
about.

"This is the sick little lad in question, I believe! He certainly does look delicate!"

The intern came forward, very professional.

"When did he fall?"

His clinical interrogation received precise replies and "yes,
doctors," emphasizing the very proper attitude of the foster
mother.

"He must be laid on the bed and undressed. I'm going to
examine him."

The little boy began to cry out in fear.

"Don't be scared!" repeated the learned young man gently. "I'm not going to hurt you."

But little Pierre called for help, his arms thrashing about.

"Aunt Lagnel! . . . . Aunt Lagnel!"

"Send the others away. There are too many people in
here!"

"Did you hear what the Doctor said? Scram! The Doctor
is going to examine your little cousin."

And the gang went meekly back to the garden. It wasn't
raining.

Side by side at the head of the bed, Laurette and Marion
craned their necks.

"Now, now, Pierrot! . . . Be quiet! . . . Let me undress you! The Doctor is not a nasty man. I'll give you a piece of sugar. Keep calm! . . . There, there . . . Do you want a smack? Aunty'll lose her temper!"

Miss Hervin stepped forward.

"Listen, little Pierre! Don't you recognize me? You don't remember what you told me last time? . . . Give me your hand . . . That's right! If you're good you'll get something beautiful. Let me show you what it is."

She turned toward Widow Lagnel.

"Go and tell the chauffeur to bring what's in the car."

"What a good idea," murmured the intern.

Seeing his foster mother go out, the child wailed.

Laurette shrugged.

"He prefers that harpy to us."

"He's three years old . . . ," remarked the intern.

Marion sprang forward. Losing its little stars, clinking and getting stuck in the narrow doorway, the Christmas tree made its appearance. She took it from the hands of the chauffeur, followed by a dazzled Widow Lagnel and the clamor of the children in the garden.

"Look, little Pierre, look! It's for you!"

The child's eyes, still submerged in tears as though in a golden pool, became immense. He made an effort to sit up.

"Look at it closely! It's a Christmas tree. You know what a Christmas tree is? No? . . . Do you see the stars? Do you see the candles? Do you see the toys? . . . And that! . . . And that!"

Swiftly his clothes came off.

"Look again! Look again, little Pierre! It's yours. Just now we'll light the candles. Christmas trees are beautiful, aren't they? Your little cousins will be coming in and you can give them what you want. Won't that be fun?"

Lying naked on the bed, having his lungs examined, his pulse examined, his legs manipulated, little Pierre said, "All that for little Pierre? . . . Really?"

"Yes, yes they are!" said the nurse. "Say thank you to the dadame!"

"Thank you, Dadame! . . . Oh, those little tops! Give little Pierre one, Dadame!"

"Just now! Just now! Don't you think it's pretty?"

"Yes, it pretty!"

"Look! You haven't seen this yet. Do you see it, under this branch?"

"What is it?"

"I think it's a whistle."

"A whistle?"

"Yes. And that, what's that?"

"It's a wa-wa."

"And that ? . . . And that ? . . ."

Marion hurried on, saying the first thing that came into her head to get the child's attention. The tree was heavy in her hands. From between the branches, which scratched at her face, she watched the baby's spellbound expressions.

"I'm finished!" the intern announced abruptly, standing up.

Marion put the tree on the table.

"Well?"

"There is absolutely nothing wrong with this child. His leg got stiff in the plaster, that's all. After his fall, he should have been gradually forced to walk; instead . . . But we're going to get him to do physiotherapy, and in a month it won't show anymore."

"Oh!" all the voices rejoiced.

"But he has a fragile, highly-strung little nature . . . He'll need . . ."

"Dadame? . . . Dadame?"

"What, my sweet?" said Marion, bending swiftly over the bed.

The baby's arms seized her neck. In her ear came a whisper filled with despair.

"Your Kissmass tree, are you gone ta take it back again?"

Marion closed her eyelids tightly over the sudden rush of tears and hid her face in little Pierre's neck.

"Take it away again? . . . Oh! How could you think such a thing? . . . You poor little thing! . . . Poor little thing!"

[XV]

The return journey under the headlamps did not inspire Laurette's pretty images. Full of practicality now, she wanted to know how the recommended treatment would be followed. Physiotherapy required a lightness of touch which one could hardly expect from Mother Lagnel. She could cripple the child by trying to go too fast. They had forbidden her to try anything until she received further orders.

"What would you do with him in my place?"

"That's a very thorny question, Mademoiselle. It doesn't look like he should stay where he is, especially in his state of anchylosis. If he were well, Lord, it might still do. That woman doesn't seem to ill-treat him, he is in the fresh air. But you saw what happened. With that band of unsupervised urchins around he could well suffer something more serious than a blow. And the medical attention he received . . . It would be useful to know the local doctors . . . We don't have time. I have to be at my hospital tomorrow morning . . . That child should be nearer Paris, under your supervision. We might be able to find another foster mother . . . Then there are the orphanages . . ."

"An orphanage! . . . That's it!" Laurette exclaimed, jumping on whatever idea came along as usual.

There followed a long incoherent interrogation to which the young man tried his best to respond.

Imperceptibly the conversation changed course. Marion said nothing.

In the outskirts of Paris the intern began to recite some poems by Valéry. As the car pulled into the garden in Neuilly, their arrival interrupted him in the middle of a sonnet by Mallarmé.

"You will dine with us!" announced Laurette. "The car will drive you back afterwards."

He did not demur. As Marion and Laurette went up to the bathroom, leaving him in the large salon, they heard him playing Debussy's *Arabesque* on the piano.

"Here's the powder, the rouge, and all the rest . . . ," Laurette said. "He doesn't play badly, that young man. But too naively infatuated with modernism. I fear he may be an indifferent snob. Here's some water for your hands."

The chambermaid disappeared.

"Laurette," said Miss Hervin. "Will you give him to me?"

"Give you what, Marion?"[1]

"Aimée's little boy."

Laurette's lips twitched up at the corners in mirth. She looked at Miss Hervin, and didn't laugh.

"What do you mean?"

"Oh! Laurette, if you only knew!"

"Marion! You?"

Laurette clasped her in her arms, holding her tight against her breast, a powder puff still in her hand. Downstairs the music stopped.

"Marion! Marion! I beg you, don't sob like that! I don't know who you are! I know nothing of your life . . . Why did you say that just now? . . . That little boy . . . Did you have a child . . . whom you've lost? No? . . . Forgive me . . . I'm talking nothing but foolishness, naturally . . . This is the first time you've been human with me . . . I love you so much!"

Marion staggered as she was led gently toward a chair where she slumped down in front of the make-up pots and the three-winged mirror. Her strange boyish face leaned against Miss Wells who stood behind her. They could both see themselves reflected full face and in profile.

"You are so beautiful . . . ," Laurette murmured as she gazed at her in the mirror.

The sobs had quickly stopped. Marion carefully wiped her eyelids, readjusting the black which had been smeared by her tears.

"Your eyes . . . Your eyes which refuse to show they've been crying . . . They're already dry . . ."

In a sweeping gesture, Miss Hervin turned away from the mirrors, bending a little so that she could contemplate Laurette from head to foot. She seized Laurette's wrists in both hands.

"Marion? What ? . . . You want me to guess everything? . . . What can I do for you, dear, dear great-hearted creature?"

The hoarse voice was particularly masculine.

"When everything is ready in my apartment to receive him, Laurette, lend me your car so I can go and fetch the child. That's all I ask of you."

With even greater delicacy, Laurette spoke so softly one could scarcely hear.

"Marion . . . I don't know anything . . . You want that little boy . . . I will give you him, of course! But you . . . It will be a heavy burden for you. Perhaps you might like it, since I was to have looked after him in perpetuity, if I provided for him . . . or . . . if I shared . . ."

"You've always been extraordinary, Laurette. But I earn a good living you know!"

She added passionately, "I'll earn even more now!"

"Listen, Marion, I want . . ."

The valet appeared at the door.

"Alas! We must go to dinner!" said Laurette, "and listen to a discussion of literature!"

Without having learned anything of the misery of Miss Hervin, without having asked any questions, she courteously stood aside to let her pass.

I still have an undamaged farm up in the north, next to the ruins of the *château*. The farmers know me only by the rent they pay. I'll say I'm a niece, or a cousin in case they know that Hervin de Valdeclare had but an only son. My birth certificate names me female, moreover, since my uncle had it changed. But the war has come and gone. There won't be anything left of the old days. If I can live in one of the outbuildings, or have some of the demolished parts rebuilt, that'll be our summer house. What revenge to create a happy childhood for a real little boy in these scenes from my own childhood! In the winter, my apartment in the sixteenth will be enough for the two of us, until something better comes along. No longer having to pay rent for my apartment on the left bank will allow me to find more luxurious lodgings in Paris. I will have an English nurse for my little boy. Nursery rhymes[2] are the seed of poetry which goes on growing for the rest of one's life.

Who could have told me that one day I would thank my uncle's memory? Had he not had the idea of changing me into a girl, none of this could have happened. What black winding paths we tread before joy!

Joy!

I can sacrifice my manly pride to joy. My motherly love will always be a little masculine, but when one holds a child by the hand, there is pride too in being a woman.

He will think I'm his mother and that will give me a sex at last. He called that woman by the name "Aunt Lagnel" and by no other. How happily my heart beat when I heard that!

I'll keep his first name. Pierre is unambiguous. Pierre Hervin de Valdeclare . . . I could adopt him immediately, I believe, but no one needs to know. In many people's eyes, I shall be seen as an unwed mother. What glory for an egg with a clear yolk! As for Ginette and company . . . We won't go into that. I'm not hard up for work with all the bandits who are looking for ghost writers. I can go back to the papers where I worked as a law student. I can even continue with my present authors. I must just make sure not to show myself, that's all.

Poor little Pierre! He also started off in life living on the fringes of what might have been. Of unknown parentage . . .

I shall be his father and his mother in one person . . . So there is a reason for my double nature.

"No!" to the voice of my childhood. "He will not become a Benedictine!"

Widow Lagnel was moved to tears, as though she would miss the child for other things than the money.

"But since he's your son, it's only natural that you should take him back! If you manage to get him to walk, he'll be a fine boy later on. And gentle as a girl, though he does have his ways at times . . ."

"Tell me something? . . . Has he been baptized?"

"I still haven't had him baptized yet!"

"Then he hasn't been. Fine. That'll be the first thing to do."

"But he does know how to say 'Gentle Jesus I give you my heart.' I've always been religious, so I have."

"Living so close to Solesmes . . ."

"Do you know the abbey? You should go in when you're passing by. It's no distance with your car."

"No, I won't go in. I don't have time. Is Pierre ready? I gave you the money—our affairs are settled . . . Here, there's some more for yourself. Yes, yes, take it! It'll be for your children's savings account. I'm sorry they're at school. Goodbye Mother Lagnel, goodbye . . . Kiss your aunt, Pierre! . . . Don't be frightened now, the car won't leave without you!"

Done up like a pudding in his peasant Sunday clothes and rolled up in his invalid blanket, little Pierre was rocked by Miss Wells's big car. Marion clasped him to her a little too virilely.

"You're hurting me, Dadame!" the little voice protested in surprise.

Mademoiselle de Valdeclare bent over her quarry. Trembling, and forcing herself to soften that voice which was stuck eternally at breaking point, she instructed, "Now, my love, you mustn't say Dadame any more. You must say Mamma."

The End

Notes

Chapter I

1. English in the original.
2. English in the original.
3. "Bobo" is a nursery word for a bump, bruise, or sore.
4. English in the original.
5. English in the original.
6. English in the original.
7. English in the original.
8. English in the original.

Chapter II

1. Neuilly is a wealthy suburb of Paris nestling between the Bois de Boulogne and the Seine. Even in verdant Neuilly, however, ghosts may walk.

Chapter III

1. The Directoire was the French Revolutionary government set up by the Constitution of the Year 3. It lasted from 1795 to 1799 and is commonly thought of as the most corrupt regime ever known. While this period was known for its extravagant fashions in dress, its loose moral-

ity, and its excesses in entertainment, directoire furniture and architecture is characterized by elongated, simple lines and sparse details based on Roman models from Pompeii.

2. Giovanni Pico della Mirandola (1463–1494) was the archetypal "renaissance man." He studied canonical law at Bologna, literature at Ferrara, and philosophy at Padua. He was a Platonist, wrote theological and philosophical treatises such as the *Conclusions* and the *Commentaries,* for which he was excommunicated and exiled to France.

Chapter IV

1. *Ecce homo! Ecce mulier!* Latin: Behold the man! Behold the woman! After his interrogation of Jesus Christ, Pontius Pilate turned to the Jews saying, "I find no fault in him." When Jesus appeared wearing the crown of thorns, Pontius Pilate announced "Behold the man!" John 19: 5.
2. "Degrés" in the original.
3. Asmodeus is known as a destroyer of marital happiness in Jewish demonology and appears in the Book of Tobit. He visited Sara as a succubus on her bridal night and killed seven of her husbands. Alain René Le Sage made him the hero of *Le Diable boiteur,* in which he and Don Cleofas fly over the rooves of Madrid peering inside the houses as they go.
4. The "baccalauréat" is a national exam for which school students sit during the last year of high school.

Chapter V

1. The French term is "le banc de maquereaux," the shoal of mackerel. The word "maquereau" is also used figuratively to mean a pimp.
2. "Une foule" is a crowd. The true feminine form of "fou" (mad) is "folle," which sounds similar to "foule." "Une folle" is also, coincidently, a queen, in the sense of a drag queen.

Chapter VII

1. English in the original.
2. English in the original.

3. The "bouquinistes" sell books along the banks of the Seine in Paris. They have their own permanent stalls built on the parapet and are especially common on the left bank in the Latin Quarter. The word "bouquin" is slang for "book."

Chapter VIII

1. The French term is "nègre," which may also be translated as "negro" or "nigger."

Intermezzo

1. *L'Ange et les pervers* was originally published in 1930, so the "post-war" years referred to are the 1920s. What we refer to nowadays, from a position of hindsight, as the inter-war years.
2. "I will make my skeleton as well as the others."

Chapter XI

1. A houri is a female inhabitant of the Muslim Paradise; hence, a volup-tuously beautiful woman. The word comes from the Arabic "hur," the plural of "hawra in hur-al-'ayun" or females gazelle-like in the eyes.
2. The lily was considered a symbol of purity, candor, and virtue. A lily growing in a lily-pot was frequently depicted in paintings of the Annunciation, where the Angel Gabriel tells the Virgin Mary that she will bear the body of Christ in her own womb.
3. The "elytra" are the outer wing cases of an insect.
4. The child's name means "Pierre Little." His foster mother's pet name "Little Pierre" is an affectionate retroversion.

Chapter XII

1. The "veillée d'armes" (warrior's vigil) took place the night before the future chevalier gained his weapons, a night spent in contemplation of

the importance of the coming day; hence, the figurative meaning of moral preparation for a test or difficult action.

2. The Thomists are the followers of Saint Thomas Aquinas.

Chapter XIII

1. The French term "grisaille" refers to a kind of painting done in monochrome grey to produce the effect of figures in relief.

Chapter XV

1. In French Marion asks "Voulez-vous me le donner?" "Le" is the direct object pronoun which is marked for gender (the object is grammatically masculine), but provides no information with regard to animacy, i.e., the hearer cannot tell whether a human being or a thing is being referred to. Laurette therefore assumes that Marion is looking for some grammatically masculine object, the comb (le peigne) perhaps.

2. English in the original.

Bibliography

Primary Sources

Delarue-Mardrus, Lucie (1900). *Le Cochon d'Inde: Mélodies pour une voix*. Charles LaGourgue, composer. Paris: Herelle et Cie.

———(1900). *Les Hibous: Mélodies pour une voix*. Charles LaGourgue, composer. Paris: Herelle et Cie.

———(1900). *Les Crabes: Mélodies pour une voix*. Charles LaGourgue, composer. Paris: Herelle et Cie.

———(1901). *Occident*. Poetry. Paris: Editions de la Revue blanche.

———(1902). *Ferveur*. Poetry. Paris: Editions de la Revue blanche.

———(1904). *Horizons*. Poetry. Paris: Fasquelle.

———(1907). *La Prêtresse de Tanit*. Play. Paris: Fasquelle.

———(1908). *Marie, fille-mère*. Novel. Paris: Fasquelle.

———(1908). *La Figure de Proue*. Poetry. Paris: Fasquelle.

———(1909, 1924, 1930, 1948). *Le Roman de six petites filles*. Novel. Paris: Fasquelle.

———(1910). *L'Acharnée*. Novel. Paris: Fasquelle.

———(1910). *Comme tout le monde*. Novel. Paris: Tallandier.

———(1910). *Par vents et marées*. Novel. Paris: Fasquelle.

———(1911). *Tout l'Amour*. Novel. Paris: Fasquelle. Reprinted 1935, Société d'Editions françaises and 1939, Tallandier.

———(1912). *L'Inexperimentée*. Novel. Paris: Fasquelle.

———(1912, 1930). *La Monnaie de singe*. Novel. Paris: Fasquelle.

———(1912). *Douce moitieé* Novel. Paris: Fasquelle.

———(1914). *Un Cancre*. Novel. Paris: Fasquelle. Reprinted 1931, Bourrelier: Editions pour la jeunesse.

———(1916). *Un Roman civil en 1914*. Novel. Paris: Fasquelle.

———(1917). *Deux amants*. Novel. Paris: Fasquelle.

———(1918). *Souffles de tempête*. Poetry. Paris: Fasquelle.

———(1919, 1928). *L'Ame aux trois visages*. Novel. Paris: Gédalge (Editions pour la jeunesse).

———(1919). *Toutoune et son amour*. Novel. Paris: Albin Michel.

———(1920). *A Maman*. Poetry. Paris: Fasquelle.

———(1920). *Le Château tremblant*. Novel. Paris: Ferenczi.

———(1920). *Les Trois lys*. Novel. Paris: Ferenczi.

———(1921). *L'Apparition*. Novel. Paris: Ferenczi.

———(1921). *Aurel et le procès des mondaines*. Current Affairs. Paris: Povolasky.

———(1922). *L'Ex-voto*. Novel. Paris: Fasquelle. Reprinted 1929, Tallandier with photographs from the film adaptation, *Le Diable au coeur*.

———(1922). *Six Poèmes d'Edgar Allen Poe*. Translation. Paris: Dépens des amateurs.

———(1923, 1924, 1929, 1935, 1937). *Le Pain blanc*. Novel. Paris: Ferenczi.

———(1924, 1930). *La Cigale*. Novel. Paris: Fayard.

———(1924). *La Mère et le fils*. Novel. Paris: Ferenczi.

———(1925). *A côté de l'amour*. Paris: Fasquelle.

———(1925, 1929). *Hortensia dégénérée*. Novel. Paris: Fasquelle.

———(1925, 1926, 1928, 1930). *Graine au vent*. Novel. Paris: Ferenczi. Film adaptation 1943, Maurice Gleize.

———(1926). *Embellissez-vous*. Essay. Paris: Editions de France.

———(1926). *Sainte Thérèse de Lisieux*. Biography. Paris: Fasquelle.

———(1927, 1947). *La Petite fille comme ça*. Novel. Paris: Ferenczi.

———(1928). *Redalga*. Novel. Paris: Ferenczi.

———(1929). *Amanit*. Novel. Paris: Fasquelle.

———(1929). *Poèmes mignons pour les enfants*. Poetry. Paris: Gédalge.

———(1929). *Les Amours d'Oscar Wilde*. Biography. Paris: Flammarion.

———(1929, 1936). *Le Beau Baiser*. Novel. Paris: Ferenczi.

———(1929). *Sainte Thérèse of Lisieux: A Biography*. Trans. Helen Younger Chase. London, New York: Longman, Green.

———(1930). *Anatole*. Roman. Paris: Ferenczi.

———(1930). *L'Ange et les pervers*. Novel. Paris: Ferenczi.

———(1930). *Le Cheval*. Essay. Paris: Nouvelle Société d'Edition.

———(1930). *Les Sept Douleurs d'Octobre*. Poetry. Paris: Ferenczi.

———(1931). *L'Amour à la mer*. Novel. Paris: Lemerre.

———(1931). *Le Bâtard: Guillaume le conquérant*. Biography. Paris: Fasquelle.

———(1931). *L'Autre Enfant*. Novel. Paris: Ferenczi.

———(1932). *Mort et printemps*. Poetry. Paris: A. Messein.

———(1932). *Le Far-West d'aujourd'hui*. Travel. Paris: Fasquelle.

———(1932). *La Quatrième Eve*. Play. Paris.

———(1932, 1933). *William the Conqueror*. London, New York: Longman, Green.

———(1933). *L'Amérique chez elle*. Travel. Paris: Editions Albert.

———(1933, 1936). *François et la liberté*. Novel. Paris: Ferenczi.

———(1934). *Passions américaines et autres*. Short stories. Paris: Ferenczi.

———(1934). *L'Enfant au coq*. Novel. Paris: Ferenczi.

———(1934). *Zrnko vo vetre*. (Graine au vent). Sv. Martin: Zioena.

———(1935). *Une Femme mûre et l'amour*. Novel. Paris: Fasquelle.

———(1935). *Eve Lavallière*. Biography. Paris.

———(1936). *Chêneviel*. Novel. Paris: Ferenczi.

———(1936). *Up to Date: Essai sur la jeunesse française contemporaine*. Essay. Paris: Allou.

———(1937). *L'Amour attend*. Novel. Paris: L'Illustration.

———(1937). *Roberte*. Novel. Paris: Ferenczi.

———(1938). *Mes mémoires*. Autobiography. Paris: Gallimard.

———(1938). *L'Hermine passant*. Novel. Paris: Fasquelle.

———(1938). *Fleurette*. Novel. Paris: Ferenczi.

———(1938). *La Girl*. Novel. Paris: Ferenczi.

———(1939). *L'Homme du rêve*. Novel. Paris: Tallandier.

———(1939). *Temps présents*. Poetry. Paris.

———(1940). *La Perle magique*. Novel. Paris: La Baudinière.

———(1942). *Le Coeur sur l'ardoise*. Short stories. Paris.

———(1943). *Verteil et ses amours*. Paris: Editions Self.

———(1944). *Le Roi des reflets*. Novel. Paris: Ferenczi.

———(1944). *Wildzang*. Antwerp, Belgium: Kroonreeks.

———(1944). *Het Ander Kind*. (L'Autre Enfant). Antwerp, Belgium: Kroonreeks.

———(1946). *El Arab: L'Orient que j'ai connu*. Travel. Lyons: Editions Lugdunum.

————(1946). *Un Garçon normand*. Boston: D.C. Heath.

————(1951). *Choix de Poèmes*. Paris: Lemerre.

————(1957). *Nos secrètes amours*. Poetry. Paris: Les Isles.

————n.d. *Rouen*. Travel. Paris: H. Defontaine.

Secondary Sources

Aurel (1927). *La Conscience embrasée*. Paris: Radot.

Barney, Natalie Clifford (1960). "Les Mardrus." In *Souvenirs indiscrets*. Paris: Flammarion, 147–186.

Billy, André (1951). *L'Epoque 1900*. Paris: Tallandier, 224–227.

Bonnefon, Jean de (1909). *La Corbeille aux roses ou les dames de lettres*. Paris: Bouville.

Cahuet, Albéric (1922). "L'Ex-voto." In *L'Illustration,* no. 4125, March 25, 1922.

Chalon, Jean (1976, 1992). *Chère Natalie Barney: Portrait d'une séductrice*. Paris: Flammarion.

Charpentier, Jean (1929). "Amanit." In *Mercure de France,* October 1, 1929, 156–157.

Descaves, Pierre (1949). "La Ronde de Lucie-Delarue-Mardrus." In *Visites à mes fantômes*. Paris: Denoël, 111–129.

Ernest-Charles, J. (1905). "Lucie Delarue-Mardrus." In *Les samedis littéraires,* vol. iv. Paris: Sansot, 227–240.

Flat, Paul (1909). "Madame Lucie Delarue-Mardrus." *Nos femmes de lettres*. Paris: Perrin, 57–97.

Gourmont, Jean de (1910). *Muses d'aujourd'hui, essai de physiologie poétique*. Paris: Mercure de France.

Harry, Myriam (1946). *Mon amie, Lucie Delarue-Mardrus*. Paris: Ariane.

House, Roy Temple, and Fritz Frauschiger (eds.) (1946). Introduction to *Un Garçon normand (L'Enfant au coq)*. Boston: D. C. Heath.

Le Roy, Paul (1936). "Colette, Lucie Delarue-Mardrus." In *Nos femmes de lettres*. Paris: Maugard.

Maurras, Charles (1917). *L'Avenir de l'intelligence; Auguste Comte; Le Romantisme féminin; Mademoiselle Monk*. Paris: Nouvelle Librairie Nationale, 202–219.

Maury, Lucien (1911). "Trois poëtesses, Lucie Delarue-Mardrus, Hélène Picard, Jeanne Perdriel-Vaissière." In *Figures littéraires*. Paris: Perrin, 297–308.

Montesquiou, Robert de (1905). "Madame Lucie Delarue-Mardrus." In *Professionnelles Beautés*. Paris: F. Juven, 51–67.

Néron, Marie-Louise (1926). "Littérature et poudre de riz." *La Fronde*, September 8, 1926.

Newman-Gordon, Pauline (1991). "Lucie Delarue-Mardrus, 1874–1945." In Sartori, Eva Martin, and Dorothy Wynne Zimmerman (eds.). *French Women Writers: A Bio-Bibliographical Source Book*. New York: Greenwood Press, 108–120.

Plat, Hélène (1994). *Lucie Delarue-Mardrus: Une Femme de lettres des années folles*. Paris: Grasset.

Pougy, Liane de (1977). *Mes cahiers bleus*. Paris: Plon.

Réval, Gabrielle (1924). *La Chaîne des dames*. Paris: Crès, 55–68.

Sirieyx de Villers, Emilie. (1923). "Lucie Delarue-Mardrus." In *Bibliographie critique, suivie d'une biographie critique, suivie d'opinions et d'une bibliographie*. Paris: Sansot.

Walch, Gérard (1914). *Anthologie des poètes français contemporains, 1866–1914*. Vol. 3. Paris: Delagrave.